The History (
Mouth of Monacacy
Oakland Mills
and
Sugarloaf Mountain
Maryland

Dona L. Cuttler

HERITAGE BOOKS
2007

HERITAGE BOOKS
AN IMPRINT OF HERITAGE BOOKS, INC.

Books, CDs, and more—Worldwide

For our listing of thousands of titles see our website
at
www.HeritageBooks.com

Published 2007 by
HERITAGE BOOKS, INC.
Publishing Division
100 Railroad Ave. #104
Westminster, Maryland 21157

International Standard Book Number: 978-0-7884-1347-6

TABLE OF CONTENTS

ACKNOWLEDGEMENTS

The author wishes to express her appreciation to Ida Lu Brown for her immeasurarble assistance in this endeavor. Thanks also to Mrs. Reeva Jones, Bob Roberson, Ellis and Barbara Roberson, John Roberson, Richard P. Brown, Mary Hertel, Connie Jones Chesley, Ross Meem and Mildred Austin for their assistance in this project. And posthumously, Eleanor Jones Bledsoe, Walker Smith, and Elizabeth Hicks Roberson. The combined efforts made the project take on a life of its own.

This book is dedicated to L. Eleanor Jones Bledsoe, catalyst for the project, who grew up in Dickerson and passed away before the completion of the final draft.

Lillian Eleanor Jones Bledsoe
January 1, 1911 - January 20, 1999

Photographic Credits

Dickerson Postal Boxes, collection of Ida Lu Brown, p. 6
1903 Dickerson Baseball Team, collection of Robert Jones, p. 7
1935 Dickerson Baseball Team, Montgomery County Historical Society p. 7
Dickerson Station, collection of Robert Roberson, p. 10
Dickerson House, D. Cuttler, 11
Train Station, Robert Tuck, p. 12
Mail Sack, Walker Smith, p. 13
Meeting the Train, collection of Bob Roberson, p. 13
Train Wreck, collection of Ida Lu Brown, p. 14
World's Fair Special, Walker Smith, p. 15
Dickerson Railroad Bridge, D. Cuttler, p. 15
Dickerson Postmark, collection of Ida Lu Brown, p. 16
Freedom Train, collection of Robert Roberson, p. 17
Train Station Fire, collection of Robert Roberson, p. 17
Telegraph office and tower, Watkins Library B & O Railroad Museum, Inc., p. 18
Store Interior, collection of Robert Roberson, p. 20
Dickerson Store, Walker Smith, p. 20
Roberson letterhead, collection of Robert Roberson, p. 21
Blacksmith shop, collection of Robert Roberson, p. 21
Roberson House, Walker Smith, p. 22
Service Station, Walker Smith, p. 23
Dickerson Manor, D. Cuttler, p. 24
Hoyle Farm House, D. Cuttler, p. 25
Nicholson House, D. Cuttler, p. 26
Jones-Gott House, D. Cuttler, p. 27
Dickerson Library and Hospital, collection of Bernadine Jones, p. 28
Nicholson House, D. Cuttler, p. 29
Williams House, D. Cuttler, p. 30
Sellman House, Montgomery County Historical Society, p. 31
Burt Nicholson House, collection of John Roberson, p. 32
Rock Hall, Montgomery County Historical Society, p. 33
Furnace, collection of Jill Chadwick, p. 34
Cabin at Rock Hall, Montgomery County Historical Society, p.34
Furnace Ford Bridge, collection of Margaret Wolfe-Aldgridge, p. 35
Tavern, collection of Jill Chadwick, p. 35
Site of Nicholson Mansion, D. Cuttler, p. 36
Hayes House, D. Cuttler, p. 37
Roberson House, D. Cuttler, 38
Bussard-Brown House, D. Cuttler p. 39
Roberson-Tobery House, collection of Robert Roberson, p. 40
Roberson House, D. Cuttler, p. 41
Dickerson Quarry, Montgomery County Historical Society, p. 43
Rose Cottage, Ida Lu Brown, p. 44
Creighton Place, Joyce Price, p. 45
Mercer Jones House, Michael Dwyer, p. 46

CHAPTER ONE

THE HISTORY OF DICKERSON

The land that became Dickerson is situated in Upper Montgomery County between Sugarloaf Mountain and the Potomac River. Although much of the land is more flat than the neighboring communities of Comus and Barnesville, several steep ridges characterize the landscape, most notably Parr's Ridge. This ridge runs east to west almost parallel with the mountain.

Early land grants in the area were: "Locust Grove," granted to Robert Veitch who built a small plaster and wood house on the property by 1780, "Nelson's Adventure" 97 acres granted to Arthur Nelson in 1739, "Ray's Venture" 150 acres granted to Luke Ray in 1743, "Largo" 30 acres granted to John Addamson in 1750, "Oversight" 58 acres granted to William Noriss in 1760, and "Bunker's Hill" granted to Nathan Hempstone. The last grant was to become the core of the community for many years. In June of 1827 William Hempstone died intestate, with eight children. In 1828 the land was divided into eight lots and the various parcels still shape Dickerson today.

Lot one included a house on "Bunker's Hill" and was $250. Lot two also had a house on "Bunker's Hill" but less land surrounding it, and was $150. Lot three also had a house on "Bunker's Hill" and had more land than the first two lots. It was $600. Lot four was advertised as having a 'mansion' and farm partly on "The Resurvey of Hanovers" and partly on "Disappointment" with 29.9 acres $3887. Lot five was Oakland Mills and 70 acres. Lots six, seven and eight were also 70 acres and surrounded Oakland Mills. At this time the road to Oakland Mills was three years old. The road from the mills to Mouth of Monocacy intersected what is now Mt. Ephraim Road at Hempstone's Store. The road was measured off on August 13, 1824 and ran eight feet from the front of William Hempstone's store.

After the road was measured, cleared and completed the following residents were remunerated for any damages to their property:

Moses Lugenbeel	$4.68	[ran Oakland Mill]
Barton Harris' heirs	$26.56	
William Bennett	$6.18 1/2	
John H. Beall	$25.75	
Eden Benson	$40.00	
John Benson	$31.25	
William Brewer	$25.31 1/2	
Joseph Jones	$25.31 1/2	
Charles Smith	$1.60	
William Hempstone	$16.33	
William H. Hempstone	$21.56	

1

The Commissioners were paid by the day:

Charles Willson	4 days $8.00
John M. Williams	4 days $8.00
John Young of Ludwick	3 days $6.00
William Chiswell	for surveying, making plat, $7.00
William Smith	1 day carrying pole, $1.00
Hanson Willson	1 day carrying chain, $1.00
Nehemiah Beuneh	1 day carrying chain, $1.00

The section of 28 that goes through Dickerson towards Martinsburg took a slightly different path, but was there as early as 1815, when a road survey for an extension towards Beallsville was filed.

William Hempstone's children inherited his land, some chose to live on it, others sold it. The eldest daughter was married to William Poole. The other children were: Elizabeth, Nathan T., Frances N., wife of William Trundle, Townley, Ann T., Christy A. and Armistead. Christy A. Hempstone married Nathan C. Dickerson, of Redland in 1834, by 1850 he had 14 slaves and a large farm. The carpenter in Dickerson at this time was Andrew M. Stephenson, he may have built the early houses, store, and other structures. In 1857 Christy Dickerson inherited part of lot number two which had 217 acres, a frame farm house, out kitchen, stable, barn, tobacco house, and other outbuildings from her brother, Nathan Hempstone. Her son, William H. Dickerson inherited what had been lot two and Christy's part of lot four. By 1858 the Dickerson farm in Redland was failing, and they moved to the land that Christy had inherited.

So, by 1860 at the crossroads was a store and several houses, with the Oakland Mills at the foot of the hill, and the Loudoun County farmers bringing their produce to the Baltimore markets along the main road of the fledgling community. During the Civil War William H. Dickerson served as a private in B Co. 35th Virginia. John Scholl was in Co. B White's Bn, Rosser's Brigade. Other area soldiers included Steve Heffner, Edward T. Moreland, Richard Poole Hays and John Whalen. But it was after the war that the town of Dickerson would boom.

In 1866 the Baltimore and Ohio Railroad Company resumed it's search for a path to lay the Metropolitan Branch. Customers wanted a shorter route west, without traveling to Baltimore first. The second section to begin construction was the Dickerson side of Parr's Ridge, laid with 60 lb. John Brown rail under the watchful eye of contractor E. D. Smith. A work camp was set up next to the track site. Between shifts, construction workers frequented Dickerson's new store. The founding of Dickerson coincides with the railroad era: 1871. By then there was a mill and granary in operation, as well as three houses and the store. The section from Dickerson's Station to Point of Rocks opened in 1872 allowing service to Baltimore for local produce, grains and fertilizer. The rest of the line opened on February 8, 1873. Formal service on the single line track began on May 25, 1873.

Four passenger trains a day ran each way, [one local] and two freight. The all-stops trains made the trip from Washington to Point of Rocks in an hour and fifty minutes. The Little Monocacy bridge was a timber trestle, terrifying for passengers to cross. Mail was delivered and sorted in a box car located on the siding; the first Dickerson Post Office. In 1873 Charles E. Scholl was president of his class at the University of Maryland School of Medicine. Local resident Henry R. Jones was appointed constable on July 10, 1877 for the Third Election District of Montgomery County, Maryland.

Passengers coming to Dickerson's Station from Point of Rocks ascended 297 feet in a six mile stretch. The grade coming in to Parr's Ridge is 1.04%—1.1% so trains often needed helpers to make it up this section. During the Depression, when hobos rode the trains, they could jump off of a front car, and get a sandwich in the store and make it back to the last car of the same train.

In 1880 a scale and elevators were built to facilitate grain loading into railroad cars. Dr. William D. Hellen was the physician and William H. Dickerson the Merchant and Postmaster. But still not many permanent houses had been built in the community, which had shifted from Bunker's Hill to the railroad bridge. By the mid-1880's the Metropolitan line carried fourteen passenger trains and five freights daily. This included the "Milk Train" and one freight with a passenger car. In 1893, 18 trains were scheduled each way. Two fatal accidents occured at Dickerson Station during this time period. Elisha Mobley was killed by a train on September 17, 1888 and Amos Reed, a B & O engineer was killed on December 31, 1889.

In 1898 William H. Dickerson opened a quarry that was a commercial boon to the community. A number of houses were built for the railroad and quarry workers on Water Street, now called Big Woods Road. All the houses on the south side of the street were built by Lawrence Baker Nicholson.

Rural mail delivery began in Dickerson in 1906 with Luther F. Loy as the first Montgomery County rural free mail carrier. Gradually the name Dickerson's was shortened to Dickerson, and the train schedules of this era reflect that change. The population of Dickerson in 1910 was 150.

In 1912 a survey was made for the Nicholson Brothers, who owned much of the land along present Route 28 near Mouth of Monocacy Road. The survey shows the present Mouth of Monocacy Road as Monocacy and Barnesville Road and Route 28 as Nicholson Street. Before Route 28 curved under the Dickerson railroad bridge, what is now Nicholson Farm Lane and Dickerson Church Road connected and extended out towards Martinsburg as Edwards Ferry Road. Harry Meem recalled that there were 14 dairy and grain farms at that time and 18 grain farms. By 1974 there were only five dairy and grain farms in Dickerson and two grain farms.

Among those from the Dickerson area who served in the first World War were Marshall Morningstar, Paul Roberson, Harry Johnson, and Grover Burdette.

In the early 1920's Harry Meem, Jr. had a summer job working for the M. J. Grove Lime Co. which was constructing Route 28 through Dickerson. He recalled riding Jones Hoyle's white mule to the job site, and was paid 25 cents a day, for a ten hour day.

In 1928 when the double tracking project was completed there were 38 passenger trains a day, which included eight locals and two all-Pullman trains. Dickerson voted by local option to be a dry area, however, locally made whiskey could be purchased at the Turner Ranch, Hildebrand Ranch, Mercer Jones and the Frederick 515 train shipped kegs of whiskey. The town physician was Dr. Charles W. Shreve, who had graduated from Georgetown and Maryland Universities. He died in 1914 at the age of 80. In 1910 Dr. R. C. Smith was practicing in Dickerson, Dr. James Hicks arrived in 1918. Life in a rural village in Upper Montgomery County had not changed so much by 1930. Russell Graham, a peddlar from Buckeystown, still came around selling Watkins Vanilla, powders, and other products.

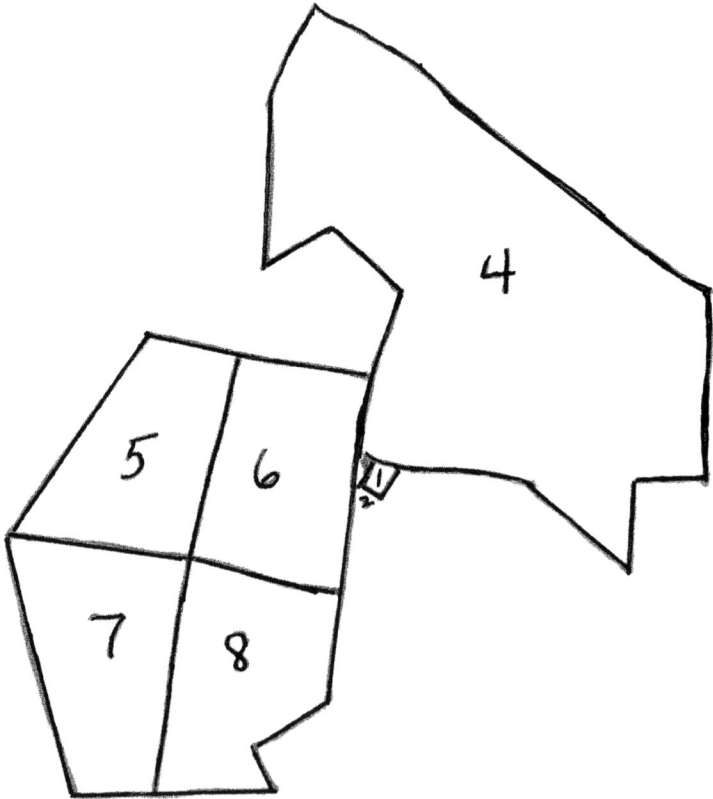

HEMPSTONE LAND PLAT

1820 TAX ASSESSMENT

Richard Beall	part of Beall's Good Will	224 acres
Eli Dorsey	part of Ray's Venture	54 acres
	Oversight	134 acres
Jesse Harris	part of White Oakswamp	245 acres
Joseph Harris	part of White Oakswamp	150 acres
Mary Harris	part of White Oakswamp	186 acres
Nathan Harris	White Oakswamp Enlarged	235 acres
Leonard Hays, Jr.	part of White Oakswamp	167 acres
Leonard Hays, Sr.	part of Father's Gift	65 acres
William Jay	part of Father's Gift	178 acres
Abraham Jones	Resurvey on Beall's Good Will	288 acres
Thomas Peters	part of Father's Gift	90 acres
John Spriggs	part of Beall's Good Will	100 acres
	part of White Oakswamp	64 acres
John L. Trundle	part of Mt. Carmel G & S mill	289 acres
Christopher Zeigler	part of Mount Carmel	30 acres

Among those who served in World War II:

William R. Baker
Joseph E. Baugher
Samuel F. Belcher
Robert Burch
Fred Cassell
Herbert Cooley
Mansfield W. Daniel
William A. Daniel, Jr.
Robert Day
Irving Dixon
Arnold Dove
Emmitt Dove
George Dronenburg
Harry N. Dronenburg
Joseph Fields
Clyde W. Foster
Dewey Sherman Foster
Hesbia C. Foster
James Goldsboro
George Hicks
Palmer Hodge
Joseph H. Hoyle
Charles Jamison
Franklin Jamison

Harold B. Jeffers
Harry M. Jenkins
William Kolb
Frank Mulligan
Baker Nicholson
Clarke O. Nicholson
Douglas Nicholson
Charles Elmer Orme
Harry L. Poole
Raymond E. Poole
William L. Rachel
Harold W. Roberson
Leonard H. Roberson
Marshal Roberson
Robert Roberson
Wilson Roberson
James Sigafoose
Earl Stottlemyer
Paul Stream, Jr.
Tom Stream
George P. Tobery
Wellstead Tipton
H. Harding Warfield
William E. Warfield

POSTMASTERS OF DICKERSON

William H. Dickerson	9 Sep 1873
James T. Umbaugh	3 May 1897
Henry L. Black	7 Jan 1901
	1902 Mt. Ephraim mail added
	1907 Martinsburg's mail was added
	1909 Mouth of Monocacy was added
Lawrence A. Chiswell	9 Mar 1914
Mary A. Jones	18 Mar 1920
Samuel Creighton Jones	1 May 1922, transferred to rural carrier
Evelyn W. White	10 Aug 1937
Roy W. Swank	17 Feb 1938
Clara B. Williams	29 Jul 1954
Elizabeth Hicks Roberson	4 Feb 1955
Charles E. Orme	20 Mar 1970
Lorraine McKimmy	1974
Joyce Wells	1 Oct 1983

Pictured below is the Dickerson Post Office c. 1942

The 1903 Dickerson Baseball team: Harry Everhart, John Luhn, Harry Meem, Sr., R. Bernard Jones, Sr., Will Luhn, Bob Jones. Front: Vernon Carlisle, Ace Harris, Algernon Padgett, Algie Slifer. Photo taken at Train Station.

The 1935 Fire Department Baseball League Team photo has the Lloyd Jones house visible, top center. Back row: Frank Hoyle, Harry C. Meem, Otis Burdette, Fenton Scarf, Earl Stottlemyer, Lloyd Jones, James Hoyle and Buck Cook. Front: Robert Williams, Pig Sears, Cootch White, Joseph Hoyle and Baker Nicholson.

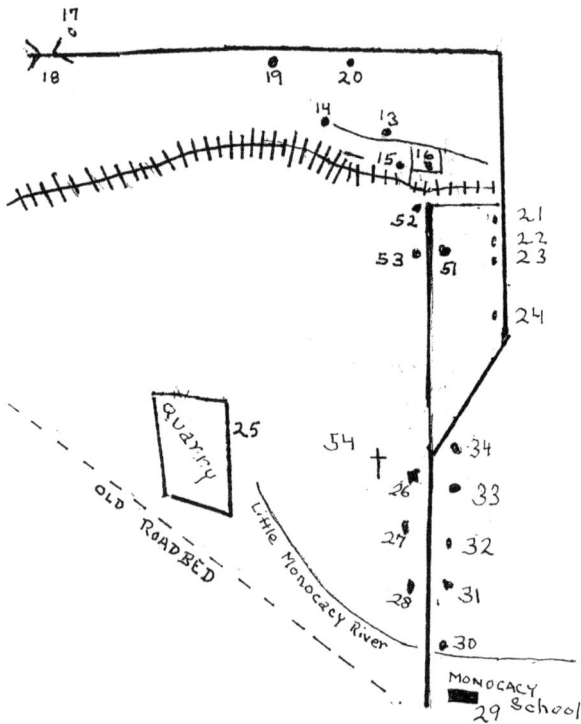

Map of Dickerson

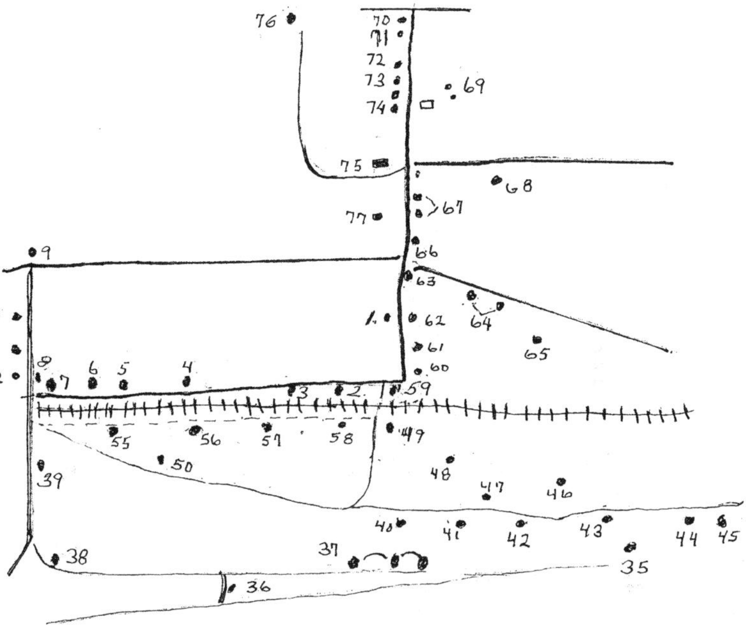

76

70
71
72
73
74

69

75

68

77

67

66

9

63

10

1. 62 64

11 8 6 5 4 61 65

12 7 60

3 2 59

55 56 57 58 49

39 50

48 47 46

40 41 42 43 44 45

38 37 35

36

CHAPTER TWO
RESIDENCES AND BUILDINGS

1. Harry Dickerson House

This property is a parcel of lot four of the original Hempstone property. William Harrison Dickerson had several children, but only W. Harry Dickerson stayed in the area. Elizabeth F. Dickerson conveyed the property to Harry in 1912. He became the storekeeper and married Mozelle Jarboe. They lived in this post Colonial-Revival house built after 1918. Currently Mrs. Margaret Lamson and her son Graham live here.

2. Dickerson Railroad Station

For nearly twenty years passengers waited for trains in the store which previously stood next to the tracks with William H. Dickerson serving as the station agent. A large brick station was planned for Dickerson, similar to the Rockville Station, but by 1891 the standard E. Francis Baldwin plans were used. The gabled window facing the tracks allowed Harry Meem, the station master, to see in both directions on the single line track, elevation 363 feet. The station was a coupon ticket office and was listed as C65 and located at mile 35.5. When the decision to double-track the entire line due to the bottleneck in this section, Dickerson was a priority, and the store had to be moved to accommodate the north bound track. Next to the station was a warehouse building, telegraph office, freight office, and "track gang" headquarters. Wesley Appleby was the railroad superintendent, and Nathan Cooley was the trackman. There were three siding tracks along this section, for grain loading, livestock facilities, and other uses and . The cars of MARC riders now fill the parking lot on work days.

In 1872 the post office was a sided box car. After 1891 the post office was located in the store. Outgoing mail was placed in a mail sack and grabbed at 10:40 A. M. as a train passed by. [top photo] Mail was also put into larger sacks and wheeled in a cart to the station to be picked up. [Lower photo]. In June 1954, when Earl F. Stottlemyer, the B & O Railroad Messenger fell ill, Charles G. Burdette was designated the mail messenger for the B & O. The mail messenger was responsible for delivering the mail from the post office to the train. Pictured below is Richard Kenton Hays.

September 24, 1942 was a foggy morning. Trains at that time were cleared by block section to move through that particular area. The Cleveland Night Express was bound for Washington, D. C. and stopped west of Dickerson that morning with a failed air compressor. A flagman was posted behind the train to signal any in-bound trains. Just seven minutes later the flagman was recalled when the compressor was restarted, and the train slowly resumed it's route. The Ambassador en route to Washington from Detroit was cleared to come through this block with a yellow light at Tuscarora. It was carrying soldiers on leave and schoolboys on their way to boarding academies. Unable to see the train ahead due to the curve, the Ambassador collided with the Cleveland Night Express at 45 m. p. h. When the slower moving train buckled from the collision, cars were hit by an oncoming freight train which was carrying rails. The resulting fire proved difficult for the fireman, as the wreckage was not near a road, and was in the cut in Parr's Ridge. Fourteen people were killed in the collision, and many were injured. The signal system was overhauled after the investigation was completed.

The 1939 World's Fair was held in New York. An English train was sent by ocean liner into Baltimore and taken by rail to New York. Many of the Dickerson folks turned out to greet the train which had to be fitted with special equipment to make the trip.

The Dickerson B & O Railroad viaduct was constructed in 1869. It is the conjunction of Route 28, Big Woods Road, Dickerson Church Road and Mt. Ephraim Road.

The 1880 train schedule for Dickerson's Station

Eastbound		Westbound	
106	6:36	107	5:36
134	8:46	141	6:48
110	2:22	109	12:13

The Queen City was one of the trains passing through Dickerson, which is located 24.3 miles from Washington, D. C. In 1935 the westbound train schedule was:

P. M. TIME	TRAIN
5:49	75 daily except Sunday
6:31	19 daily
6:54 F	77 daily except Sunday
7:19	37 daily except Sunday
9:04	1 daily
11:54	9 daily
12:47	117 daily except Saturday and Sunday

Eastbound train schedule

A. M. TIME	TRAIN
4:16	118 daily except Saturday and Sunday
5:14	10 daily
5:43 F	38 daily except Sunday
6:27	18 daily
6:50 S	2 daily
7:05	78 daily except Sunday
7.44	20 daily
7:53	6 daily

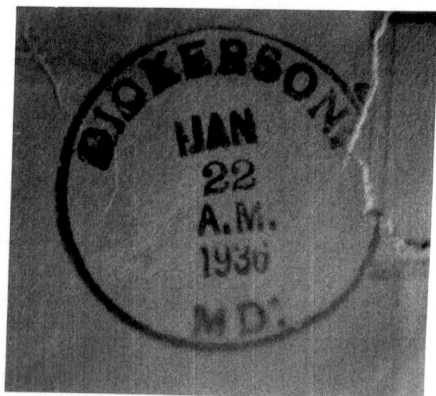

Top: For the 1976 Bicentennial, the "Freedom Train" passed through Dickerson. Below: The architectural focus of Dickerson was extensively damaged by arsonists in 1982. It was restored in the late 1980s with state and county funds.

3. Telegraph and Tower

Harry Meem had learned telegraphy from his uncle in Gaithersburg. He came to Dickerson in 1891 and boarded with Mrs. Frederick O. Sellman, after accepting the position of station agent and telegrapher. Meem married Nora Sellman, daughter of Frederick, and had a house built where he raised a family. He remained the station and telegraph agent for 45 years. The interlocking tower was added in 1906 and the telegraph call was DN. Here Meem set signals and moved the track switch by mechanical devices. He had a worksheet where he recorded the passing trains and manned the telegraph instruments not only for railroad business, but also for Western Union. Listed in the 1900 & 1910 census as telegraph operator was William Henry Sears.

4. Dickerson Store

Constructed originally of logs, the center portion of the store was built for William H. Dickerson to supply the railroad camp c. 1870. After the construction workers were gone, the general store continued to serve the local farmers and residents. In 1890 the store was moved to make room for the new station and in 1891 the post office was moved inside the store. Mr. Dickerson was the postmaster until 1895. In 1910 the store was moved when the road was widened, and it was moved again in 1928 when the double track was laid. Bean Hallman, a barber from Mt. Ephraim, came several times a week to offer his services. Mort Ambush was another barber at this location. R. Kenton Hays clerked here and teased the children who came in on errands. One remembers asking for a pound of sugar and he quipped "the sour kind or the sweet kind?" Puzzled, she replied, "whatever Mother usually gets." Fannie Carlisle Ensor recalls seeing Gordon Strong here picking up his mail, reminding her not to buy candy. Robert T. Dayhoff bought the store in 1945 and had an addition built. Major Barton of Thurston ran the store after 1950. Mr. Mobley and later Pedro Mejias operated the store until it was discontinued in the 1970's. The structure to the right of the store was used for storage.

In 1906 Luther F. Loy was the first rural free delivery man in Montgery County. The Dickerson Post Office continued to be located in the store until the addition was added to the Dickerson Market. The interior photo shows Earl "Sox" Stottlemyer and Ellis Roberson in the store and pictured below are Earl "Sox" Stottlemyer and Roy Swank.

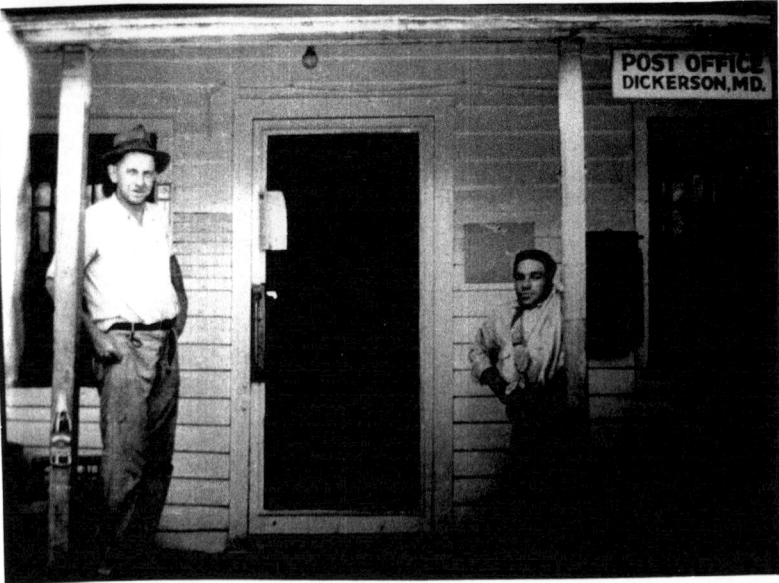

5. Site of the Blacksmith Shop

Benjamin F. Roberson, pictured below, moved to Dickerson from Barnesville and operated a shop across the street, until it burned down. This second shop was built circa 1916. In addition to shoeing horses and mending buggies, a blacksmith made nails, hinges, trivets, andirons, and many other goods. The shop housed the bellows, forge, anvil, and workbench, as well as tubs of water for cooling the metal.

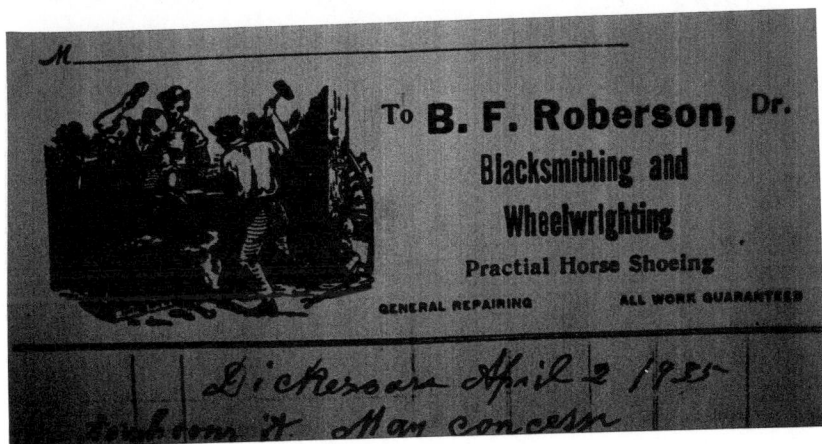

To **B. F. Roberson,** Dr.
Blacksmithing and
Wheelwrighting
Practial Horse Shoeing

GENERAL REPAIRING   ALL WORK GUARANTEED

6. William Roberson House

This Colonial Revival style house was built for Will Roberson at the turn of the century. Lee Purdy did the stonework and foundation, and the lumber came from Brunswick. Mr. Roberson and his brothers did much of the carpentry work themselves and Piney Day worked with them. The house sits on property called "Ray's Venture" granted to Luke Ray in 1743.

7. Roberson Garage and Filling Station

Howard and Will Roberson ran the Gulf filling station. Pictured left to right are Ben Roberson, Walter K. Matthews, Howard Roberson and William Roberson. In 1906 William Edgar Roberson and Howard C. Roberson formed the partnership of Roberson Bros. Plumbing and Heating, and also operated the filling station. Currently the plumbing business is operated by Ellis Roberson and sons.

8. Dickerson Manor

Originally part of "Ray's Venture" granted to Luke Ray in 1743, the 1850 census lists Zadok and Mary Hemston [sic] farmers, with seven children here. When Christy Hempstone-Dickerson inherited this property from her brother, Nathan, there was a log cabin and several outbuildings on the 217 acre property. The cabin had several additions over the years. William H. Dickerson inherited the land and the Baltimore and Ohio Railroad condemned part of it for the Metropolitan Branch in 1872. In addition to keeping the store and being the postmaster, Dickerson farmed the land near the house, and sold off other lots in parcels. William Dickerson lived here, followed by two of his daughters, Robert T. Dayhoff owned this house, and sold it to Roy Swank. Paul Stream and his family were occupants before Kerrie Kyde, who currently lives here.

9. Will Hoyle Farm

In the 1840's through the 1880's Richard A. Harding had a large farm located on this property, which extended across present-day Route 28 to where this house is now situated. The Shreve farm adjoined this property and Louis B. Scholl owned this parcel of the property until 1909 when William Linwood Hoyle and his wife Mary Nellie Jones Hoyle purchased the land and ran a dairy farm. They had four children, and two maiden Aunts, Mollie Jones and Aunt Emily J. Clements living here. The rear addition is one-story enclosed porch. James B. Runkles was the next owner, and he sold it to Mr. and Mrs. Robert T. Dayhoff. Bernard and Emma Williams lived here in the 1970's and 80's and worked for the Dayhoffs.

10. Elizabeth A. Nicholson House

This house was built in 1924 after Mrs. Nicholson inherited several parcels of land in Dickerson. Even after electricity was installed, construction was delayed for several years waiting for perc tests to give the needed results. Other occupants include Edward and Naomi Chiswell and the Cunninghams. The Cunningham's daughter Evelyn married the boy next door—John Gott. Ken and Phyllis Strite are living here presently.

11. Jones-Gott House

This Colonial Revival house with hipped roof was built circa 1919 by Willie and Claude Nicholson. Claude's wife Ella died before the house was finished and he died shortly thereafter. The house was sold to Lawrence B. and Lillie Nicholson Jones about 1920 and then to Brooke and Nellie Gott who swapped houses with the Jones's. The Jones family moved into the old stone house at Gott's Mill and the Gotts moved here. Charles Coleman and Mary Phiban are living here now.

12. Dickerson Hospital

Dr. Alfred McGill Belt purchased this lot to build the Dickerson Library and Emergency Hospital. In 1904 this lot was purchased from Damaris Sellman, and a 1912 survey show the location of the proposed building. Dr. Belt was the grandson of Alfred Belt who purchased Rock Hall on the Monocacy River. When he envisioned a hospital for Dickerson, he did not know that the land wouldn't percolate. He died during the 1918 influenza epidemic and never saw his dream become a reality.

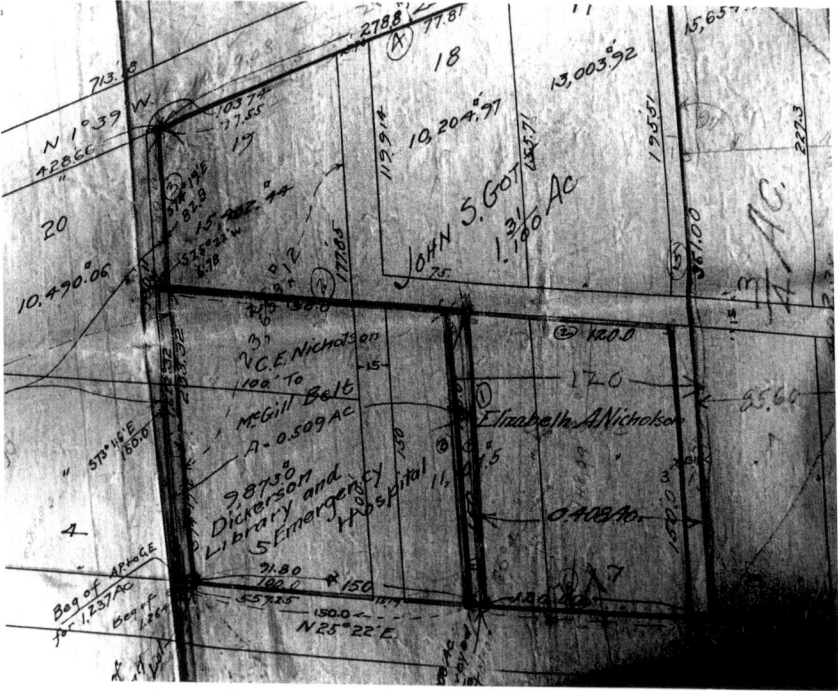

13. Nicholson House

Built for Susie Oland Nicholson and Arthur P. "Bake" Nicholson circa 1900. They had three sons and Arthur died in 1919 after contracting the flu. Susie raised the boys alone on an income derived from selling her baked goods at the Women's Market in Bethesda. Nathan Hildebrand lived here with his sister Anna Mae, through the 1960's and then the Palmer family moved here. Presently the Leonard Carlson family lives here. The rear addition is two-stories with a side door.

14. Nicholson-Hicks-Williams House

This property was part of "Veaches Loss" 42 acres granted to William Courts in 1770. The house was built circa 1895 by Lawrence Baker Nicholson for Lawrence Jones. The road leading to the house was called Jones Road on the 1912 plat. Hattie Susan Hicks moved here from Mt. Carmel and Miss Sally Walker lived here, too. In 1928 Leo Roberson installed radiators: three down stairs, including the bathroom, and three upstairs in the bedrooms, and two in the attic. In the early 1950's Elizabeth Painter rented the house and then Charles Douglas, a railroad employee, and his family lived here from 1955-1959. Woodbridge and Bea Williams have lived here since that time.

15. Old Sellman Boarding House

Frederick Sellman's old boarding house formerly stood next to the livery stable. The boarding house was run by his wife, Damaris, and served salesman, quarry officials and other tradesman. When Frederick Sellman retired from farming and his store at Mouth of Monocacy, he raised horses and ran the livery stable, renting rigs and also ran a race track around a path bordered by Jones Road, Nicholson Street [now Route 28], the lane to the boarding house, and the roadway in front of the stables. In the middle of this track, the first blacksmith shop had been operated by Thomas Nicholson. Sellman died in 1904 and Damaris began selling off parcels of their vast holdings before she died in 1912 and the boarding house was gone soon afterward. The barn had stalls on the first floor and a long hall which was later converted into bedrooms after the boarding house was gone. Later it was converted into a house for Sadie and Jones Hoyle, who maintained the road from Dickerson to the mountain and ran the Carpenter Standard Co. Other occupants include the Thomas' and Smiths, but two bulldozers demolished the old home in 1960. The Dickerson Automotive Center now occupies the space, and the warehouse is operated by Harland Shoemaker.

16. Burt Nicholson House

On the site of the first blacksmith shop, the last of several homes built for Linwood Burton "Burt" Nicholson was here, this one was built circa 1949 on land purchased from his brother, Arthur P. "Bake" Nicholson. Burt's widow Carrie Roberson Nicholson lived here and the house was taken down in the 1970's. One of Burt Nicholson's previous homes is behind the site of the Dickerson School. It was built c. 1927 as a honeymoon cottage. Following the wedding, all of the school children turned out to see the bride and groom arrive in their new home.

17. Rock Hall

This tract was granted for 1,002 acres to Orlando Griffth in 1712. Roger Johnson purchased this property on May 15, 1795 from Francis Deakins. It was used in conjunction with the Catoctin Furnace at Thurmont, by supplying pig iron from "Bank Ore." Roger Johnson operated the furnace here until 1829. The two-story house was built in 1812 of local stone with eighteen inch thick walls, handcrafted mantles, two inch thick doors with iron hinges stretching across the entire door, iron locks with brass knobs, old brass knocker and a gabled roof. Joseph A. Johnson, son of Roger, lived here. The addition is one-story and adjoined the summer kitchen. Slave cabins were chinked logs with stone chimneys, and the overseers house was frame. The forge produced 12 to 15 tons of pig iron a week by extracting surface deposits of bank ore along the banks of the Monocacy River. Charcoal was supplied from charcoal makers on Sugarloaf Mountain. The pig iron was taken by cart to Bloomsbury in Thurston to make bar iron. A road was constructed from Rock Hall to Bloomsbury [now Wellcome Farm] for a more direct path between the two Johnson properties. The partnership of the Johnson Brothers was dissolved in 1793. The demand for this quality of iron ore decreased in the 1820's as better grades became accessible. The property was sold in 1830 to Dr. Alfred Belt and remained in the family until 1939. Dr. Belt had in his possession a contract from 1819 between Roger Johnson and David Moody for charcoal at one and a half cents per bushel. In 1850 Daniel Price was still operating the woolen mill here. The remains of the race for grist mill are still visible, but the miller's log house washed away in the flood of 1889. A large one-piece Stile stone used for mounting is still located out front.

The forge, pictured below, was about 30 feet square at the base and was built of sandstone quarried farther upstream. The fire pot was about eight feet across. In addition to the furnace stack were other buildings: casting houses, store houses, two lime kilns, distillery, charcoal store house, and worker's cottages. The furnace required 400 cords of wood turned into charcoal per week to operate.

18. Furnace Ford Bridge

The top photograph taken in 1905 shows the bridge over the Monocacy River that replaced the one downstream which was destroyed in the 1889 flood. In 1930 this bridge was torn down, and until the new bridge was completed Rev. E. Wilson Jordan had to be rowed across the Monocacy for church services at Forest Grove. The present bridge consists of three steel camelback through trusses, each 145 feet long, set on concrete piers, completed in 1931. The Tavern was run by the Dixons and later Edith Spahr, and was a stopping place for thirsty travelers and locals. It closed in 1976 and is no longer standing.

19. Site of the Nicholson Mansion

Of the Hempstone land grant, this was lot four or "Pretty Spring" and part of "Beall's Good Will." A large brick mansion was built for Richard and Jemima Harding and purchased by Dr. William D. and Nancy Johnson Hellen in 1878. Later the home of William O. Sellman, the stately brick mansion was purchased by Lawrence Baker Nicholson who left it to his son Charles in 1904. Piney Day was living here when the house caught fire and burned in the early 1930's. A modern home and horse farm are now located here operated by Bert and Edna Lytle.

20. Hayes House

The center section of this house was built by Linwood Burton Nicholson circa 1930. Additions have been built on to each side by Ben Hayes. Daniel and Mildred Piasecki here now. From the stream crossing the property one can retrace the past to shanties that housed quarry workers. Some of the residents were Silvro Albensen, quarry foreman, and Lawrence Price, William Redmond, George Walters, Andrew Mellon, and John Walker lived in dwellings that are now gone.

21. Howard Roberson House

Built in 1907 by Charles B. Sellman of Poolesville for William Edgar and Rosa Mae Virts Roberson, they sold the house to brother Howard Calvin and Mary Elizabeth Bussard Roberson in 1912. This Colonial Revival style house features chestnut trim used because it was inexpensive and plentiful after the chestnut blight of 1904. Gerard and Yvonne Mulgrew live here now and she tends a beautiful garden.

22. Bussard-Brown House

Built in 1905 by Charles B. Sellman of Poolesville for Henry and Elizabeth Bussard, George D. and Kate Bussard Brown lived there afterward. Elizabeth Hicks Roberson stated that she and husband Leo Roberson were living in this house in Dickerson in 1934-9 and were paying the highest rent anywhere at $12.50/month. In the late 1950's and early 1960's Harry Dronenburg lived here, and the store across the street built. Wade and Edna Stowers lived here until recently when Edna Warfield Stowers sold the house. Robert Zarnetske and Shirley Taylor are living here at the present time.

23. Roberson-Tobery House

When Benjamin F. Roberson's sons moved to Dickerson to open a filling station, he sold his shop in Barnesville, and moved to Dickerson soon afterward. This house was built for him in 1913. After his death in 1935, his son-in-law and daughter, George B. and Marie Louise Roberson Tobery continued to live here. Donald Roberson owned this house until recently. Now Bob Oram is living here.

24. Paul Roberson House

This cottage style house was built for Paul and Mary Roberson circa 1919. Mary continued to live here with their daughter June through the 1940's. The house has one and a half floors and Andrew McDermott and Lila Turner currently reside here.

25. Dickerson Quarries

The D. C. Quarry opened in 1898 on part of "Beall's Good Will." The smaller of the two quarries at 17 acres was owned by the D. C. government, and it supplied bluestone for curbs in Georgetown, and crushed stone for the water filtration plant. Some of the workers were listed in the 1900 census: Clinton M. Rhodes, Raymond L. Weatherly, a driller, John Cox, a blaster, George W. Turner, stonemason, Thomas Kohlenburg, Lloyd Jones, engineer, Jesse Hellock, and Richard Collier. The small quarry closed in 1905. The larger quarry was originally part of the 20 acre tract "Doe Neck" granted to Daniel Veatch in 1764. It was purchased by William H. Dickerson and sold to Standard Lime and Stone and later the Bakers sold it to Otto Anderson when he came to Montgomery County in the 1930's. Later owned by Mary P. Anderson, the 451 acre quarry opened in 1900 with seven workers and closed in the 1930's. This quarry shipped crushed rock for railroad beds. The rock was locally referred to as "trap rock" which was dark colored, fine grained igneous rock. Leo Roberson worked in the quarry from 1918 to 1921. Amos Thomas was the weigh master and Mercer Jones was the superintendent. The quarry employed 30 workers at it's zenith, six days a week from 7:30 AM until 4:30 PM. Men received from $2.00 - $2.50 per day. There were houses down near the stream where Italian workers lived and tended the mules at night. These houses, which included foreman Silvro Albensen 's house, were taken down after the quarry closed. Each worker had a tract or section to which they were assigned. Stones were loaded in the carts, pulled by mules to the incline. Here the cart was attached to a cable, and when the boss signaled, the cart was pulled up the incline by a boiler. There were seven 100 horse power boilers supplying steam power to operate the crushers, hoists and incline. At the top of the quarry, the stones were crushed, sorted and dumped into railroad cars. When 10-20 cars were full, the Brunswick station would be called for a locomotive to pick up the cars. Some stones had to be dynamited, at which point the men would wait in the dynamite shack for protection from the blast. Two pumps ran continuously to keep spring water out of the quarry. Occasionally windows of nearby residences would crack during charges, or from debris, and repairs were paid for by the company. One holiday weekend the pump attendant got intoxicated and fell asleep, and water came in too fast to save any of the equipment. The gas motor which ran the pump ran out of fuel too long to rebuild the pressure. Carts, incline sections, and steam shovels are immersed in 90 feet of water. Other out buildings include a blacksmiths shop, a boiler room, crushing building, pump house, and stable.

Dickerson Quarry

43

26. Rose Cottage

When Lawrence Allnutt White retired from farming at "Linden" in 1919 he had this house built. Lawrence and Annie Oliver Belt White moved in 1920. The front fence was covered with pink Dorothy Perkins roses, from which the name was devised. Off the center hallway are three bedrooms and a living room. The small kitchen is in the rear with an adjoining dining room. Mrs. Annie White Everett and Mrs. Evelyn White Grey lived in Rose Cottage after they became widows and spent their later years here. One of the outbuildings remain, and Mark Badgley, current owner, recently remodeled this house in the 1990's.

27. Creighton Place

Built for Samuel Creighton Jones in 1923 by Will Dudderar of Urbana, and Clagett C. Hilton dug the well. This house was the first in Dickerson to have electric lights using a Delco generator. Mrs. Jones designed the house after her brother's house in Alexandria, Virginia. The house features a large central foyer on both floors, a living room and bedroom on the south side running the full-length of the house, dining room and breakfast room on north side, with kitchen and powder room in the center. They also had a wall telephone in an oak cabinet. Twelve people were on a party line from Buckeystown. Later, a Dickerson exchange was activated, but calls still went through Buckeystown. Mrs. Beulah Nicholson Jones intended to run a tourist home, so the rooms were nice and large but when a large number of guests were staying here, the children slept on pallets on the floor. In 1922 route 28 was under re-construction. Mrs. Jones wanted the road to pass in front of Creighton Place, and she was successful in getting the road re-routed. Mrs. Jones also taught piano lessons for fifty cents. At one time a small store and gas pump were located near the road. They raised chickens and sold eggs and had a garden on the side, with a round brooder house in the back. Presently the Joneses grandson John F. Price lives here with his wife Joyce Byrd Price and daughter Kathryn Price.

28. Mercer Jones House

Lloyd S. Jones purchased this property from Warner Sellman February 25, 1845. The house was originally constructed of logs. When the front addition was built, c. 1890, the entire house was weather boarded. It had a water tank upstairs that was connected to the nearby windmill for power to pump. The house had nice marble fixtures and was the home of the quarry foreman. During Prohibition Days one of the residents had a still on the property, and he received a warning that he was about to have official guests. By the time the county authorities arrived, there was not much liquid left. From the house on the hill across the street, several of the neighbors watched the raid. Otto Anderson purchased the house in the 1930's. Fred Parks is the current occupant, Bill Anderson is the owner.

29. Site of Monocacy School

Land for the Monocacy School was donated by the White family in 1864. John Scholl was the first teacher in this one room 24 x 30 school. Other teachers include: Mr. Settle [1874-5], L. R. Gost, John S. Gott [1900], James F. Burns, Alice Spates, Miss Dugent, Elizabeth and Ara Lee Hicks. The school was damaged during the Civil War by the U. S. Army, and $75.00 was appropriated for repairs in 1865. In 1913 Poole's Tract School was closed and the students were consolidated with the Monocacy School. In 1918 the Montgomery Sentinel carried this item: "Monocacy School News; Twenty-nine books were purchased for the school library with funds raised at the Hallowe'en Social by Elizabeth Jones. The school has organized a Red Cross Auxiliary Chapter, with Betty Jones, treasurer, Miss Alice L. Spates, teacher, Mildred Chiswell, secretary. They have raised $8.25 by holding a Patriotic Entertainment." Pictured in the photo are: Evelyn White, Elizabeth White, Maurice Chiswell, Raymond Webster, Arthur Webster, Edwin Sellman, Annie White, Evelyn Brewer. Back row: Miss Dugent, teacher, Pauline Hays, Marian Sellman, Lawrence Jones, Newton Brewer and Lee Jones. The second picture shows two of the Roberson boys in front of the school.

Children walked to school carrying their lunch bucket. The road was not paved at the time of this photo which was taken near Windmill Hill. After the school closed in 1921, the materials were used to construct an outbuilding on the F. Malcolm White farm where the school bell is now located. The following page shows the last class to attend Monocacy School 1919-1920. Back: Michael Bender, Louise Shreve, Edna Chiswell, Irving Fisk, Elsie Lee Chiswell, Rosalie Jones. Second: Edward Wootton, Blanche Wootton, Eleanor May Jones, Helen Jones, Virginia Jones, L. Eleanor Jones, Bernadine Jones. Third: Lloyd Jones, Carroll Fisk, Norman Wootton, William Jones, A. Jones, Jr. Front: Turner Wootton, Earl Shreve and Lawrence Eaton.

30. Mt. Carmel

Francis Deakins was granted "Mt. Carmel," 433 acres and added 97 acres of "Nelson's Adventure" to his holdings. John Veatch purchased the combined property and it was conveyed in four lots to his children in 1759. Thomas Veatch received 124 acres of "Mount Carmel" and raised his family here. The house consists of four stone sections and one frame section. It is made mostly of sandstone and is two-story with a gable roof and double end chimneys in the east gable. A one-story Victorian porch runs the length of the frame section. The slave quarters' chimney has a date of 1833 on it, and the grist mill was constructed around the same time. The mill was in operation until 1910, and had wooden gear shafts to turn the millstones to remove the bran which was fed to livestock, while the flour was sold locally. The mill was built of sandstone and ironstone obtained on the property and water from the Little Monocacy River turned the overshot wheel. A trough carried water back to the creek. The mill race ruins are increasingly harder to find. Millers here include: M. Richard Gott, Lawrence Baker Jones, Lee Hicks, and Gilbert Roberson. The property passed to Veatch's daughter Mary who married M. Richard Gott, Jr. In the winter of 1862 while Mary Gott was away, the overseer was running the mill and supervising the slaves. During a storm three Union soldiers came on to the property. They beat on the door demanding admittance, and overseer David Carson sent young John Gott upstairs and retreated to the living room. The soldiers had imbibed moonshine whiskey before their arrival and proceeded to knock out the window between the kitchen and living room. As one of the men was coming through the window, Carson shot him dead at point blank range. The other two battered down the kitchen door, got rough with the slave women, and Carson sent them to their quarters, which angered the soldiers. The soldiers became violent, knocking out most of the windows with sabers, or shooting them out. One of the other men fired at Carson and missed, the bullet remains in the dining room window frame, near where he had been standing. This soldier was captured and court-martialed. Carson sent two of the slaves to the commander in Poolesville to report the incident. On September 6, 1862 the Army of Northern Virginia crossed the Potomac River five miles below Mt. Carmel. Elijah White, Mrs. Gott's son-in-law was serving as a staff captain and invited his commander, Thomas Jackson, to dinner at Mount Carmel. The family had very little notice to prepare dinner for their guests, and tables were set out on the lawn. Not wanting her guests to be kept waiting for their meal to be served, Mary Gott returned to the kitchen to inquire why the food was not being brought out, and found the soldiers helping themselves to fried chicken, ham, potatoes, corn, squash and blackberry pies. The Gott grandchildren often re-told this story by ending it, "General Jackson rode off telling the Gotts that the soldiers needed it more than he did," so it was the time that Thomas "Stonewall" Jackson did not dine at Mount Carmel. The second story was added after the war, when repairs were being made. Years later the house was uninhabited and deteriorating. It was purchased in 1968 and restored with new paneling, windows, and other repairs. Mrs. Kit Hallambauer is the present owner.

31. Jones House

Parceled from "Nelson's Adventure" which was patented for Arthur Nelson in 1739, the present house was built c. 1925 by Linwood "Burt" Nicholson for Lawrence Beall Jones. Other occupants include the Jacques, Miss Chevallier, her sister and husband, and then Mr. & Mrs. Sinclaire. Alan and Patricia Knight are the current occupants.

32. Windmill Hill

John W. Holland had this house built c. 1886 and sold it to Elizabeth Ann Nicholson. Dr. James Hicks, pictured below, lived here c. 1918-1930. He had come to Dickerson to begin his retirement, but when he arrived, so did the influenza epidemic. He continued practicing medicine during his years in Dickerson, and also had a farm at Bunker's Hill. This property was about 8-10 acres, and was unsuitable for large scale farming because it was swampy. William Wallace and Sarah Shields are living here presently.

33. Chiswell House

Built c. 1921 after the new road opened up this area for houses. Edward L. "Ned" and Naomi Chiswell lived here in the 1930's and 40's and then the Supplees lived here. The Economos lived here, and then Mark and Laura Longsworth purchased the house recently.

34. Hughes House

This house was built for Upton K. and Emma Hughes c. 1903 by Lawrence Baker Nicholson. Their daughter, Mrs. Upton, was a school teacher, and lived here with her mother and sons David and Everett after Mr. Hughes died. John Vinson, a quarry laborer, boarded with the family. W. Thomas and Margaret Jones Kessler lived here until recently when the house was sold to James Nesbitt. There were formal English gardens in the back of this house many years ago. The first floor of the house has a living room, dining room and kitchen with two bedrooms on the right.

35. Wolfe-Jones House

Part of "Beall's Good Will," this property was conveyed from William P. N. Lawson, Zachariah and Martha Cooley to Lawrence Baker and Elizabeth Nicholson in 1900. Elizabeth sold it to Jesse Hyatt and Laura Dorcas Hyatt Wolfe in 1904. The house was built shortly thereafter. In 1909 Reginald Bernard Jones purchased the house and land for $2,400. The house has had several additions and the front and back porches have been enclosed. In the attic beams are stamped "ship to R. B. Jones, Dickerson." In 1959 Charles Garrett Cooley enclosed the porch, and added a kitchen for the Jones'. The home remains in the family and is called "Jamboree."

36. Gregg Cottage

Edgar "Jellybean" and Evalina Duvall Gregg had this cottage style home built in the early 1930's. It was parceled from the R. Bernard Jones property. Peter Winslow lives here now, and his wife Dana is an artist. She is using one of the outbuildings for a workshop and another for storage.

37. Three Houses

These houses were built by Lawrence Baker Nicholson prior to 1900, and were intended for area workers of the railroad, state roads, quarry, etc. The first house was the home of Richard and Grace Hoyle Cromwell, purchased in 1914 from Willie S. Cooley. Later Charles White and Raymond "Bub" Poole lived here. The middle one was purchased by Walter K. and Eleanor M. Luhn Matthews, who operated milk wagons from behind the house; first pulled by horses, later trucks carried the milk. W. A. Hardy lives here now. In the third house was Harry Everhart and then William C. and Rose Etta Roberson Baker. Later Walter Baker and his son Henry were house painters and lived here. Brad Lowery lives here presently. The old road ran behind these houses, through the front yard of "Jamboree" and on down toward Gott's Mill.

38. Sears House

A typical Maryland house, this frame house features a center gable with rounded window, and front porch the length of the house. Built by Lawrence Baker Nicholson for Nathan S. Cooley in 1900. Cooley was a railroad employee and was married to Lillie M. Sears. Her brother William Henry Sears and wife Airy V. Duvall Sears lived here, too. In the 1900 census he is listed as a telegraph operator living with them. William and Airy purchased the house in 1924. Sears retired December 1, 1937. After his death, Airy and her daughter Marge continued to live here until the 1950's. Jean Findlay lives here presently.

39. Dickerson Market

Built circa 1946 by Edgar Grubb for Harry Dronenburg, Dorothy Dronenburg operated Dronenburg's Store. Pictured are Dawn Foster, Martha Stream, Irving Dixon and Joe Deadrick. This was later converted into a house where Will and Rose Baker and later Lorraine McKimmy lived. It was torn down in 1997 for additional parking space for Pedro's Store, which was later operated by Arthur Stull as "Stull's Grocery." Ralph Thacker was the next merchant at this location and prepared and sold coffee, soups and sandwiches for the customers. He named the enterprise "Dickerson Market" and carried a full line of groceries. The current store features a grill, convenience items and a salad bar and is owned by Buck Fowler. The Post Office moved in to the addition in 1960. There are 146 boxes rented; two rural routes with 554 customers. Presently there are six employees: One postmaster, two clerks and one rural carrier-auxiliary.

60

40. James Belcher House

Built c. 1900 on what was then called Water Street, now called Big Woods Road. Designed for rental houses for the railroad, quarry and state road workers, Lawrence Baker Nicholson built these houses from the same set of plans. In the late 1940's James Belcher moved here from another house on this street. Michael and Carol Oberdorfer live here presently.

41. Stottlemyer House

Built c. 1900 by Lawrence Baker Nicholson as rental property Richard Collier was here in the 1910 census, stone quarryman with his wife and four children. Harry Stottlemyer who worked for the state roads lived here later, and his widow Mildred still lives here.

42. Poole House

Built c. 1900 by Lawrence Baker Nicholson for rental property, 1910 lists Truss Thomas here an inspector with wife, child and boarder. Walter Poole, who worked on the railroad lived here after 1920. Current resident Deborah Wolf has an art studio in the back. There had been a similar house next door built c. 1900 by Lawrence Baker Nicholson for Claude and Ella E. Nicholson. They sold it on February 14, 1912 to Luther F. and Jessie Hilton Loy. Her mother Mary also lived here with them. The house is no longer standing. Before becoming the first rural free delivery man Mr. Loy worked for the railroad. His mail route included a section in Frederick County as well as Montgomery County. He lived in Dickerson for 35 years, raised Lee and Edgar Smith here and died in this house in 1936. Afterward James Alonzo and Jane Padgett lived here, and then Walter K. Matthews purchased the house. It was rented to Jess Gossard, followed by Walter Cochran who was living here when the house burned down.

43. Padgett-Morningstar House

Built c. 1897 by Lawrence Baker Nicholson. Joseph A. Padgett is listed here with his family in the 1900 census. The house was sold to Marshall and Annie Morningstar and then to Larkin Yates. Mrs. Anne Yates still lives here. Down the road past the creek was Oscar Copeland, the shoemaker.

44. John Holland House

The center log portion of this house was built circa 1850. John W. Holland owned this property in the late 1800's. His sons Boyd and Ernest lived here and ran the ice plant. Mr. Stottlemyer lived here c. 1900. James Belcher lived here in the 1930's and operated the Ice Factory. Presently Warren and Dorothy Warfield live here.

45. Holland-Runkles & Matthews Ice House

Built c. 1880 to store ice which was cut on the Little Monocacy River and kept here in blocks. Originally the mill race ran right beside the road and a water wheel supplied power to keep the ice cool. Boyd and Ernest Holland worked here when their father John W. Holland owned the ice plant. At that time the ice was delivered by horse and buggy. There was also a cider press here. Horse pulled wagons delivered apples to be processed here, but the cider was not sold here. After Walter K. Matthews and James B. Runkles purchased the Ice Factory in the 1930's, they had a diesel motor installed. Ice was then delivered by Diamond T pick-up truck to customers and stores in Dickerson, Comus and Sellman.

Dickerson, Md.,

™ **Runkles & Matthews,** ᴰᴿ·
Manufacturers of Ice

46. Rhodes House

Prior to 1900 this house was built for John C. Rhodes by Lawrence Baker Nicholson. A native of New York, Rhodes was a Sargent in Co. K, 91st NY Volunteers in the Civil War. He was a member of the building committee for the Mt. Pleasant M. E. Church, South and represented the church at many Quarterly Conference Meetings. His sons William, Joseph, Oscar and Clinton Rhodes lived here and repaired model-T's and other automobiles in their garage. They were also blacksmiths. In the 1900 census Joseph is listed as a coachman, and Clinton as a quarry laborer. The 1920 census lists Clinton as a farm laborer, and Oscar as an automobile mechanic. Oscar Rhodes' widow lived here for many years, before the property was purchased by Jim Stull and rented to Donnie and Nancy Rowe.

47. Carlisle-Roberson House

Built by Lawrence Baker Nicholson c. 1899, [1920 census has Harry L. and Viola B. Selby Carlisle here, he was a painter] Robert and Gaye Roberson lived here later. Followed by Norman and Alice Thompson, Mr. Mobley in 1957 who ran the older store, and then sold to Tina and Russell Smith.

48. Dickerson School

The Monocacy School was aging, and the students needed a school built closer to the town. In 1920 Dickerson requested $25,000 from the School Board for a new building. They got $11,780. The property was purchased from Zachariah and Martha Cooley. The school was built of brick and had two stories with a basement. When it opened in the fall of 1921, high school classes were offered, but due to low enrollment these classes were discontinued five years later. Mrs. Beulah Jones and Miss Emma French, principal, got the Community League started and financially supported the school with monthly meetings, minstrel shows, lectures, dances and entertainments by students. The League purchased a piano, athletic equipment, milk and clothing for several needy families in the neighborhood. In 1925 a Delco generator added lighting to the school and a water pump was installed, together costing $800. The graduation services in 1925 were held in the school auditorium for Jacqueline M. Darrieulat, Lester R. Bell, and Lloyd J. Jones, Jr., the diplomas were presented by Prof. Edwin W. Broome, Superintendent, and addresses were given by Miss Darrieulat and Mr. Jones. There was vocal and instrumental music and Miss Emma French, principal, presided. In 1928 Miss Aud was the teacher and Mr. Mullinix was the principal. In 1932 Miss Kathryn Soper came to Dickerson School. The two-floor building had four classrooms with additional rooms in the basement which had been used for shop classes, and housed the toilets. It took 27 years to get plumbing on the second floor. Miss Soper found old home economics equipment in the basement, and decided to set up a cafeteria, staffed by parent volunteers. There were two coal burning stoves, and some dishes. She requested a cabinet, that was delivered with mice and holes, so she refused to allow it to be installed. The delivery men left the health hazard on school grounds until Miss Soper threatened to have it burned if it was not removed. School lunch was eventually served with food donated from parents. Miss Soper married S. Creighton Jones and after Mr. Jones died she married Charles C. Crone. Mrs. Crone made many other improvements in the school. She is pictured on the following page on May 3, 1959 when the school burned to the ground. Pictured with Mrs. Crone at the fire is Ross Meem. The students and Mrs. Crone were sent to Germantown. Some of the other teachers over the years were: Mrs. Bishop, Marie Keesee, Frances Meem, Marjorie Chiswell, Dorothy Todd, Virginia Fyffe, Ara Lee Hicks, and Owen Knight, principal. Pictured in the school photograph of 1947 are: Top Row, Jane Burdette, Elizabeth Stream, Joe Straughan, John Roberson, Philip Bell, Peter Dowell, Second, Eveline Brown, Myrtle Young, Jane Marie Starkey, Calvin Cooley, Douglas Burdette, Elsie Smith, Third, Lee Smith, Doris Gue, Barbara Grimes, Charlotte Wilson, Jimmy Catron, Carlton Stottlemyer, Front, Carol Sue White, Wade Stowers, Jr., Russell Smith, Mary Ellen Gibbs, Jon Clark, Peter Gum, Patsy Stottlemyer, absent: George Stream.

49. Meem House

After purchasing part of the Dr. Charles N. Worthington farm from William P. N. Lawson this house was built for station agent Harry C. Meem, Sr. and his wife Nora Gittings Sellman Meem in 1904 by Charles Sellman. It is a two-story Colonial Revival and remains in the family. Harry Meem was the first person in Dickerson to own an automobile. He purchased a Ford Model-T touring car in 1912. The front porch has been enclosed. Granddaughter Lael Meem Scott and her husband Robert Scott live here now.

50. Trundle House

This small house was the home of John S. Hallman, a slate quarry worker, and then Horatio Trundle lived here. It is one of the older homes in the neighborhood. Washington "Bill" Hamilton lived here after Mr. Trundle. He was the town electrician and handy-man, but he had no electricity or plumbing in his own home. Bill lived here through the 1960's.

51. Tobery-Roberson House

Part of "Oversight," 58 acres granted to William Norris in 1760, this house was built c. 1913 for George B. and Marie Roberson Tobery. Frank and Iva Ruffner Roberson were the later owners. Other occupants include Leo and Elizabeth Hicks Roberson [1927-28]

52. Hays House

One of the few brick houses in Dickerson is this Colonial with Federal detailing. It was built by Richard Poole Hays in 1882. Hays clerked in his father's store in Barnesville until he enlisted in the 35th Virginia Cavalry. In 1875 he married Betty G. Batson in Barnesville. He purchased ten acres of "Beall's Good Will" from Richard Harding and had the house built on fieldstone. The bricks were brought from an old house in Barnesville which had been taken down. Some of the beams have a store named stamped on them. Over the front door is a four paned transom and two on the sidelights. The door is set in a segmentally arched doorway with brick keystone. The windows have louvered shutters which repeat the arch of the window frames. Each room was still heated separately by stoves when Richard Kenton Hays was living here. Leroy Jones was boarding here in 1918. Edgar and Evalina Gregg lived here and did carpentry work when Mrs. Ellen Imrie came to live here in 1942. She had fireplaces installed and other improvements made. In 1953 Pete and Sally Dilanardo purchased the house from the estate of Richard Kenton Hays. In 1991 the original tin roof was replaced with a copper roof. Two other homes were on the property. One was a small two or three room house with no plumbing or electricity where the Lutz's lived and grew Talbott lima beans. The only trace of the other dwelling is the foundation. In the photo, notice the large turkeys in front of the steps.

50. Leroy Jones House

This property is a parcel of "Beall's Good Will." The house was built practically right on the main road in 1900 for quarry worker, Eugene Philip Jones. His son, Alfred Leroy, and daughter-in-law Lottie Cornwall Jones lived here after Eugene moved to Gaithersburg. Gilbert and Grace Roberson lived here and had the rear addition built when plumbing became available. Martin Wiseman married Anna Roberson and lived here before Edgar Gregg and Evalina Duvall Gregg who lived here while caring for Richard Kenton Hays, and then moved in next door when he needed more assistance. In 1943 Mrs. Ellen Imrie purchased the property and had the house moved back from the road. At that time, Frank Martin was living here. The front porch was later enclosed.

51. Dickerson Methodist Church

When the Mount Pleasant M. E. Church needed extensive repairs, the congregation voted to build a new church closer to town. This property was originally called "Oversight" and the 58 acres were granted to William Norris in 1760. The land for the church was donated by John H. Baker of Buckeystown Standard Lime and Stone Company for $5.00 with the stipulation that no cemetery or burial ground ever be put there. The building committee consisted of Howard Roberson, Frank Padgett, Luther Loy, William Roberson, Walter Baker, George D. Brown, Walter K. Matthews, William H. Sears, James B. Runkles, Dora P. Wolfe and Rev. Charles Reiter. The cornerstone was laid in the spring of 1930 by Poolesville Masonic Lodge 214. The contractors were Piney Day and Jess Gossard, with the men of the church donating their time and energy. The congregation had $500 toward the building from church extension, and mortgaged $1,600 with the loan repaid in 1942. Rev. E. Wilson Jordan dedicated the building. The wooden chairs were replaced with pews from W. T. Alexander and Son, for $500. A church in Washington, D. C. that was replacing their windows sold the old ones to Dickerson, but they were replaced in 1953 with leaded stained glass memorial windows. In 1962 Dickerson withdrew from the Clarksburg Charge, built their own parsonage and joined with Koontz Chapel on Park Mills Road. In 1972 an electric organ was given in memory of David H. Brown.

Clarksburg Circuit Preachers:	Dickerson Charge Preachers:
1930-31 E. Wilson Jordan	1961-63 Joseph C. Rial, Jr.
1932-37 S. James Dulany	1963-67 M. Robert Mulholland
1938-45 Thomas Morgan	1967-70 Richard A. Watters
1946-47 Charles Shaffer	1970-71 Wally Shearburn
1948-53 Jack G. Ammon	1971-73 R. Gwinn Lacy
1954-58 Ben F. Hartley	1973-76 Mark S. Hathorne
1959-60 Howard L. Allwine	1976-85 Miriam H. Jackson
1960-61 L. W. Burton	1985-89 Mark Kimpland
	1989-89 Diane Rainey
	1989-91 Charles Sellner
	1991-93 Mary Jo Simms-Baden
	1993-95 Valerie Wilson
	1995- Susan Hunt

52. Nicholson-Cooley House

Lawrence Baker Nicholson moved from Comus, and purchased two and three quarter acres from Charles Worthington in 1892. He moved his mercantile business here, and built a store which he operated until his death in 1904. The two and a half story frame house was built on a fieldstone foundation in 1893 and features a beautiful stairway with turned balusters and carved Newell posts. The house was sold to Zachariah Cooley, when he moved here from near Comus in 1896. Cooley died in 1928 and his son William S. sold the house to Claude O. Cooley in 1931. Charles and Vivian Orme lived here in the late 1930's. The outbuildings include a one-story curing shed on a log foundation, corn crib, and another shed covered in siding. Other occupants include: Raymond C. Cooley, Owen Knight and family, Gilbert & Grace Roberson, Mary Roberson and then Eva Heffner owned this house from the 1960's to the 1980's. James Goldsboro was a resident here until the 1990's. Marshall Coates lives here at the present time.

53. Chiswell House

The land was parceled from "Ray's Venture" which was granted to Luke Ray in 1743. This house was built c. 1880 for Captain Lawrence A. Chiswell, who was the second store owner to the adjacent mercantile. The house was later owned by William Cooley, Algernon Padgett, Lawrence Baker Nicholson, and John Fyffe. Charles Otho and Vada Knill Roberson lived here from the 1932 to the 1980. Their daughter Dorothy relates that the mail bag was tossed into their yard from the train, daily. Claude and Donna Belcher live here presently.

54. Nicholson-Chiswell-Jones Store

When Lawrence Baker Nicholson moved his business here from Comus, he built this store c. 1882. Lawrence A. Chiswell became his partner, and took over the business after Nicholson's death in 1904, purchasing it in 1909. Maurice Chiswell was the third merchant here. S. Creighton Jones moved here from Mt. Ephraim, and became a partner in the store, eventually running it himself. The Talbott lima bean was grown in Dickerson and attracted people as far away as West Virginia to come and buy this variety. The Dickerson Post Office was located here from c. 1927-1932. The cause of the fire which destroyed the store on December 23, 1932 was never determined, but firefighters had no water reserve to fight the blaze with until a railroad tender car could be sent from 18 miles away. The store was the discussion place for politics, weather, news, etc. and sold fresh bread from Frederick, groceries, meat, beans, salted fish, sugar, candy, dry goods, and fresh local eggs. Eighteen to twenty milk wagons brought milk to the store, and loaded up with local merchandise to sell in Frederick.

55. Lawrence A. Chiswell House

This house was built for Lawrence A. Chiswell c. 1914 by Lawrence Baker Nicholson. S. Creighton Jones and his family lived here from 1918-1921 while their new house was under construction. Maurice Chiswell lived here from about 1923-1933, and then the Jacques, and later Leo Roberson purchased the house in March 1939 for $1,000 down from Mrs. L. A. [Hattie] Chiswell; total price $2,750, which included six acres. The Robersons had five sons, a cow, chickens, a hog and a garden. Mrs. Elizabeth Hicks Roberson canned about 400 quarts of food annually, had their own milk and eggs, and got along very well in this house, except for the termites. It was sold to Bill Moore. Heather Rae lives here also, and they combined their names when naming the property Brae Farm.

59. Mercer Jones and Sons Granary

The property was purchased from Henry Scholl on November 17, 1858 by Lloyd S. Jones. Built near the railroad, a siding track was here for loading ground corn via funnels into railroad cars. When cars were full, they were coupled to a freight train for shipment. The granary was operated by Mercer C. and Lloyd Jones, and they also sold feed and grain, and bought wheat and corn from local farmers. In later years Lloyd sold farm machinery and became an International Harvester Dealer. In the 1960's the business was discontinued, the building was abandoned when the lower photo was taken in 1970. When Neutron purchased the property, the granary was torn down.

60. Jones House

This house was built in 1906 for Lloyd James Jones, Sr. and his wife Elizabeth Eleanor Brosius Jones on property which had been parceled from the Henry Scholl property in 1858. The Harry J. Kelly family purchased it from the estate of Mr. Jones. The house was converted into office space for the Neutron plant which is now located next to the house.

61. Peddicord-Algeo House

Part of the original Dickerson property, this land was sold by Elizabeth E. Dickerson to George and Vallie Runkles in 1910. Two years later they sold it to James and Marion Runkles who sold it to Hammond and Thomas Peddicord January 28, 1914. The house was built in 1915 for Thomas and Grace Peddicord. Mr. Peddicord was a postal clerk in Dickerson in the 1920's and lived here through the early 1950's. John Jackson, a congressional speech writer, lived here from 1952-1962 and sold the house to Leon and June House, who sold the house c. 1975 to the Hazards. Currently William and Inge Algeo live here.

62. Runkles House

After James B. Runkles purchased the farm which was located behind this house, he had this bungalow style house built. James owned and operated a saw mill, a spoke factory, and farmed the land behind this house. Other owners include Charles Jamison, who purchased the house in 1941 for his parents to live in, and Elam J. and Bea Supplee. Mr. Supplee taught math at Poolesville High School and lived here from 1950 - 1978. Ronald Geddes purchased the house in 1978.

63. Dayhoff House

When Robert T. Dayhoff moved from the house across Mouth of Monocacy Road, he had this house built of oak. The timber was cut on the farm in the 1930's. He farmed the land after Dr. James Hicks and the Roberson's [1917-late 1930's], and his daughter married Arthur Jay Johnson, who owns the farm currently. When Luther Renneberger moved from Comus, he came to live in this house. William Sutphin is living here presently. The house across the street is the home of Bobby and Lutie Dayhoff. Thirty acres of the property were purchased from C. Milton Dickerson in 1947.

64. J. Clayton Hoyle House

Two houses were built on adjoining lots in the 1920's that were similar in construction. J. Clayton and Anna Holland Hoyle lived in this house. Arthur Johnson owns it and has tenant farm workers there presently. In the other house was Harry Stottlemyer until the 1930's when he moved to Water Street. Then Tom, Grover, Otis, John and wife Helen Burdette lived there. Harry Mulligan lived across the road, but the structure disappeared after the last resident, James Earp, moved. He was a B & O Railroad track walker.

65. Site of the Black-Runkles farm

There used to be a lane to this farm between the Runkles and Peddicord homes.
Mr. Runkles spoke factory made wagon spokes and his saw mill cut railroad ties
and other lumber. The farm was purchased by Henry L. Black on August 23,
1900. Previous owners include William Hilton, who sold it to Richard Beall.
Thomas O. White's widow Huldah White sold it to Henry L. Black, Dickerson's
third postmaster. At the time of the sale, the farm boarded the properties of Mary
Mullican, Thomas Reid and Mary Plummer. Henry Black later started what
became the Embassy dairy in Washington, D.C. After James B. Runkles bought
it, he had tenant farmers in the house. The Creagers were followed by Bill and
Evelyn Burdette who were there when the house burned to the ground in the
1940's. After Mr. Runkle's death, the property was sold to Maloney Concrete, as
Maloney hoped to use the area while building PEPCO. However, Maloney lost the
bid on the job, and the property sat idle until J. Maurice Carlisle and Ralph
Thacker purchased, and sub-divided the property.

66. Runkles-Dayhoff Farm House

This land grant was originally called "Bunker's Hill." Henry Scholl lived here in the mid 1800's. His son Louis B. Scholl sold this parcel of the property to W. Harrison and Mozelle J. Dickerson. The Dickersons sold to Pinkey and Sarah Lomax in April of 1920. James R. Hicks and William H. Lawson each bought part of the property in 1921. Dr. Hicks operated the farm from 1917-1934 at which time his son Leo and wife Elizabeth Hicks Roberson took over the farm. In 1935 James B. Runkles bought it. A brick house replaced the old frame house. The farm sold to Robert T. Dayhoff, whose daughter Peggy married Arthur Jay Johnson. Elizabeth Hicks Roberson relates that the former house here was a Sears Roebuck house put together by Arthur P. "Bake" Nicholson. The present brick house was built in the 1930's.

67. Site of Mount Pleasant M. E. Church, South and Cemetery

Mt. Pleasant Church construction began in August of 1887. The building committee included James Maxwell, Zachariah Cooley, J. W. Collier, George William Bitzer and John C. Rhodes. One acre was purchased from James and Sarah Frances Beall Maxwell for $75 on March 3, 1888. The church was constructed for $120 by William T. Hilton of Barnesville. The men of the church hewed all the timbers which saved $1.50 per day, per man. The dedication was held on Sunday June 24, 1888 and the Forest Grove congregation also attended the service conducted by Will Hammond. The Trustees were: Benjamin F. Roberson, William A. Luhn, George D. Brown and Henry L. Black. In 1899 the Trustees purchased an additional one-fourth acre of land from Henry C. and Laura V. Lawson to be used as a potters field at a cost of $55.10. Gordon Strong's sister Ella was married here. By 1925 some younger members of the congregation wanted to relocate the church in the town of Dickerson. When extensive repair work was needed in 1929, the congregation voted to move, and build a new church. The old building was sold to Ernest Page and Mr. Moxley who used the lumber for barns and outbuildings on their farm.

Mount Pleasant Cemetery
* denotes tombstone was moved to Monocacy Cemetery in Beallsville.

Andrews, George J. 18 Sep 1901 70 years
    w Lucretia E. d. 4 Jan 1894 42-20-8
Bussard, Henry 25 Feb 1915 78-1-27
    d Hannah 18 Sep 1891 0-5-0 [by Elizabeth]
Cecil, Ira Herbert 29 Jul 1905 - 9 Jun 1906 s/o Wilbur E. & Ann E. Sears Cecil
Cooley, Amos J. 5 Aug 1827 - 5 Aug 1907
    w Elizabeth A. 28 Mar 1836 - 6 Dec 1916
Cosgrave, Frances C. 1886 - 1932 w/o William D. moved 27 Nov 1941 *
    d Rose Marie 1911 - 1913 moved 27 Nov 1941*
Cosgrave, Joseph W. d. 6 Dec 1903 71-8-20
    s Charles F. 10 Sep 1888 - 16 May 1911 by Alice
Dixon, Calvin S. d. Jan 1919 moved on 18 Sep 1935 *
Dixon, Grover Cleveland 6 Nov 1885 - 1 Sep 1906 s/o William & Elizabeth
Edwards, Catherine J. 1 Jul 1846 - 13 Mar 1887 w/o David
Jewell, Marie M. 21 Apr 1935 "lived six hours"
Keith, Charles T. 15 Dec 1871 -
    w Florence Z. d. 2 Jul 1898 31 years
King, Emmeline Price 20 Dec 1837 - 18 Jun 1898 w/o Walter
Lenhart, Elmer 31 Aug 1913 - 20 Sep 1914 s/o Eugene & Laura
Luhn, George Christopher, Sr. 17 Aug 1820 - 22 Jan 1896 *
    w Annie Elizabeth Sellman Luhn 26 Nov 1825 - 22 Jun 1911 *
Luhn, Sarah Catherine McLain 23 Mar 1857 - 10 Aug 1880 w/o Chas. A. Luhn *
Maxwell, James Stevenson 20 Sep 1844 - 3 Aug 1892 h/o Sarah Frances Beall*
    d Maggie Blanche 12 Dec 1877 - 21 Jun 1895 *
Miller, James S. 1933 - 1934
Mobley, Laura 2 Aug 1904 39-4-25 w/o Mahlon F.
    s Arthur 4 Jun 1900 - 26 Jul 1918
    s Frank 6 Dec 1888 - 12 Mar 1915
    s George 9 Mar 1911 27-5-9
    s Henry 18 May 1903 18-4-24
Mobley, Mary J. d. 3 Mar 1918 82-4-13 w/o John
Montgomery, Baby 1966
Moreland, Edward T. Co B. 35th Bn CSA 2 Oct 1841 - 19 Dec 1909
Mossburg, Infant d. 1 Aug 1895 d/o Samuel & Ida V.
Nichols, Harriett Lucretia 1863 - 1909 w/o Charles E.
Nichols, John R. age 75
    w Rose A. 23 May 1874 - 31 Jan 1912
Nicholson, John 1 Aug 1893 53-5-4
Price, Children of W. D. & Sarah F.
    d Lula F. 30 Aug 1890
    s Charles N. d. 17 Aug 1894 1-0-14
    s Daniel F. d. 16 Sep 1898 0-10-16
Price, William H. d. 13 Apr 1896 69-2-2
    Ann R. 16 Dec 1830 - 17 Oct 1907

Redmon, Lash 1878 - 1958 [Elisha Redmond]
     w Mollie E. J. Bussard 1885 - 1944
     s Redmond, Arthur 29 Mar 1920 - 29 Apr 1940
Rhodes, John C. Sgt. Co K 91 NY Vol 27 May 1841 - 29 Jul 1905
     w Catherine E. 15 Feb 1847 - 29 Jun 1928 "Our Mother"
Richardson, Mary E. 6 Apr 1902 4-4-16 d/o James L. & Mary E.
Rinker, Alice V. 8 Sep 1877 - 4 Jul 1909 w/o Samuel P.
Rinker, Margaret V. d. 20 Apr 1905 7 months d/o Samuel P. and Virginia A.
Selby, Annie S. R. 12 Dec 1887 - 29 Jan 1906
Selby, Jessie M. 1 Feb 1908 2-5-2 d/o G. W. & H. H.
Shumaker, Carrie 20 Feb 1889 - 23 Apr 1909 w/o W. S. Shoemaker *
Studebaker, Rebecca d. Mar 1921 *
Thompson, William H. 21 Apr 1861 - 26 Sep 1902
     s. C. Dempsey 27 Jun 1895 - 2 Dec 1902 [by Nettie G.]

68. Lawson House

Zachariah G. and Martha Johnson Cooley bought several parcels of the extensive Henry Scholl property in 1866. Scholl had purchased this section from Elizabeth Offutt. This parcel was sold on November 18, 1867 to Henry C. and Laura V. Lawson. In 1899 they acquired additional property on the other side of Barnesville Road, which was later incorporated into the Ensor farm. At the bridge over the Little Monocacy River was Daniel Price's grist mill. When the B & O Railroad purchased property near Oakland Mills, the road was diverted to the site of the old mill and renamed. Other occupants include: Will and sister Addie Lawson, Matilda Duvall, Mrs. Tillie Littell the artist, c. 1932-34 who gave political dinners and provided entertainments while her Barnesville chateau was under construction. Later Eveline, Earl and Newt Stottlemyer lived here, then Bill Burdette followed by Paul Streams in the mid-1930's. This house is currently the home of J. Maurice "Bo" Carlisle.

69. Harris Farm

"White Oakswamp" was divided between Jesse, Mary, and Joseph Harris. Nathan Harris added to his portion, naming it "White Oakswamp Enlarged." He had 235 acres in 1820. The log cabin is now covered in plaster or stucco and has had at least three additions.   Built c. early 1800's, the exterior chimney was later incorporated into one of the additions.   Alfred, Charles and Harvey J. Harris, inherited the land from their father. Perched atop the ridge is the two-story house with a center gable built c. 1870. The front section is of log construction and the ell is frame.   Along the front is a two-story porch to catch the breezes from Sugarloaf.   An exquisite example of the German bank-barn is located on the property.   The Watkins family lives there now.

70. Mt. Ephraim Store and Post Office

The general store at Mt. Ephraim was built by Ephraim Gaither Harris, who served as the postmaster from August 4, 1882 until December 13, 1888. The store was there before 1861 when Harris began selling whiskey to the Union troops who were manning the signal stations on the mountain. Harris was worth $5,279 by 1867 and employed a full-time cooper, David M. Haynie, and established a blacksmith shop here.   In 1888 Reverdy Dronenburg became the postmaster following Harris' death, and subsequently married his widow, Ida Justina Zeigler Harris of Hyattstown. Mail service was discontinued October 16, 1902, and the property divided in 1910. The store was sold to S. Creighton Jones in 1912. Bean Hallman, a barber from Banner Park Road, styled hair on the front porch of the store. In 1918 the store burned to the ground, but portions of the foundation are still visible. In the late 1920's a store was built between here and the Turner house at the corner behind this property. Will Turner operated a store on the corner of Banner Park Road and Mt. Ephraim Road. Mary Ann still lived in the home beside the store in the 1910's, but only the front steps and pump remain today. The land now belongs to Stronghold, Inc. and is used for scouts and equestrian events.

71. Mount Ephraim

The Harris family had owned this land for several generations. Ephraim G. Harris chose this location for his home and purchased the parcel from his father Abraham in 1868, and hired builder William T. Hilton to build a house next to his store. The house was named after it's owner, who, due to his imposing stature had been nicknamed "Mount Ephraim." Built from local materials, the clay for the bricks was hand-pressed and fired on site. The slate for the roof was quarried on the adjoining farm. White pine, oak and chestnut were taken from woodlots on Sugarloaf Mountain. The house originally had a one-story front porch with a center gable, but it was removed when the house was extensively remodeled in 1941. Fortunately, the two-story porch on the back was retained. It faces south to catch the summer breeze and winter sun. The present living room was previously a kitchen and has a deep fireplace/laundry out building, but the smoke house has been demolished.

Following Mr. Harris' death, his widow married Reverdy J. Dronenburg. He added to the property by purchasing two adjoining farms, the William G. Baker farm in 1902, and the Clinton Moore farm in 1903. The family continued to live here until 1912 when it was sold to Lawrence Baker Nicholson. C. Beulah Nicholson Jones purchased the 5 72/100 acres for $10.00 on August 12, 1912. S. Creighton Jones, her husband, ran the store, and she taught English and music at Halstead School. He had a car with solid rubber wheels before getting a Detroit. The Joneses rented rooms to other teachers at Halstead, and to family members coming to visit boys in Mr. Strong's care. Mrs. McCormack stayed with them, as did the Chestnuts. Miss Amy Shank and Eleanor Miles boarded during their tenure at Halstead. Mrs. Jones also taught piano lessons at home.

In April 1919 the house was sold to Francois F. and Marie Louise Darrieulat who had come from France in 1893. He was an Olympic fencing instructor who was training Gordon Strong in cycling, rowing and fencing. He ran a camp behind the house in the summers and also had a dry cleaning business. There were big vats for the dry cleaning chemicals behind the farm and a barn with large double doors for ventilation.

In 1940 Frederick Gutheim purchased Mt. Ephraim, after it had sat vacant. Architect Julian E. Berla prepared the remodeling plans, removing the Victorian trim and adding modern conveniences. James VanDien is currently residing here.

72. Frye House

This land was originally part of "Hopewell" but was given to John Noress' son George as "Father's Gift." The house was built for Mason and Mamie Carlisle Frye c. 1905 and later was the home of son Herman Leon Frye. They had been living next door with her parents in the 1900 census, so this was probably parceled from that farm. Mason was a 12 team driver, and owned this farm in 1910. There was a blacksmith shop at Mt. Ephraim run by Adolphus Lindig and son Henry. The Lindig home was across the road, but is gone now. The Lindig land had been purchased from Henry Griffith.

73. Carlisle House

One parcel of "Father's Gift" was "That's It." As early as 1850 James A. and Christiana Spalding Carlisle were living in a previous dwelling here, with the Spaldings next door. In 1872 the property was sold to George J. Andrews by Susanna Hardy. In 1902 Richard C. and Frances Appleby Carlisle purchased the property, but the house was built previous to this date. The youngest of their children was then three years old. The Carlisle children attended Poole's Tract School along with their neighbors. In the 1910 census Harry Carlisle is listed as a mail carrier; he was later a local farmer but his house is no longer standing. During World War I Richard C. Carlisle purchased some property across the road near the Little Monocacy Creek from Leonard Hays, who was at that time serving in France. The deed had to be sent to Paris for his signature, but when it could not reach him, it was signed by the consulate. In 1920 Richard Vernon Carlisle purchased this property and sold it to Harry and Frances Carlisle Ensor in 1959. The barn across from the house was built in 1931. This land was once part of the Henry Lawson farm. The field beyond it was part of "Father's Gift" which Luther Albert Ballenger purchased from John T. Price in 1908. The Ballenger house was a frame two-story house which was sold with the farm to Richard Vernon Carlisle by Luther, Ernest and Lillie Kinna Ballenger in 1920.

74. Duvall House

A parcel of "Resurvey of Father's Gift" called "That's It" was sold by George J. Andrews to Isaac T. Jones in 1874, who sold it three years later to Henry and Elizabeth Bussard. The house was built for them c. 1878. In 1884 they sold the property and house to William D. and Malinda E. Duvall. William died in 1901, and Malinda lived here until 1932. The house was sold by her six children in 1934 to J. Maurice Carlisle for his sister Lucy who lived here until 1958. Down the hill behind this house was the old William Hallman house. Charles H. Johnson from Martinsburg married the Hallman's daughter and was living here by 1910. Several of their daughters worked as domestics in Dickerson. The old house was torn down and replaced by a modern house.

75. Poole's Tract School

In 1877 a school was requested and the Montgomery County School Board appropriated $375 for the new building which was constructed on a parcel of "Largo." Poole's Tract opened in 1879 and was insured for $450 in 1883. In 1900 the teacher was Franklin A. Pearre followed by John A. Luhn. Some of the students here in 1900 were: Gracie Collier, Mary E. Collier, William F. Collier, Ann C. Collier, Isabel E. Collier, Beulah L. Collier, Ruth L. Collier, Franklin L. Dronenburg, Ernest H. Dronenburg, Agnes Clements, Raymond Cooley, Louisa Cooley, Carrie Fon, Gabriel Lawson, Adelbert Lawson, Raymond Lawson, Nathan Hildebrand, Annie Hildebrand, Bertha Hildebrand, Allen Carlisle, Harry Carlisle, and James Maurice Carlisle. The 1910 teacher was Mary H. Shreve. It was closed in 1913 and the students attended Monocacy School. Nathan Cooley purchased the building in 1921 and used it as a barn. His former residence on the adjoining property is currently being demolished.

76. Luhn House

George Christopher Luhn, Sr. and his wife Anna Rebecca Sellman Luhn came from Germany to Middlebrook [near Germantown, Md.] in 1850, and then purchased a large piece of land behind Scholl's Hill on June 10, 1884. Their five sons were wheelwrights and the family was active in the Mt. Pleasant M. E. Church, South. The house was two-and-a-half stories with a center gable, and an addition in the back. It has been vacant for many years. Also on the property is the ice house, wheelwright shop and barn. Mac Luhn and Harry Carlisle were paper hangers. Not far from here were the two quarries used in the construction of the aqueduct. In 1828 the first rail lines in Maryland were laid from the nearby quarry using twelve to sixteen feet long pieces of oak with a wedge cut diagonally to the center and fitted with strap metal. The wheel of the car fit into the groove and the ties were ballasted with rock. No cross ties were used, and the route was never graded. Flatbed cars were supported by iron wheels and axles with two horses pulling each car. One wheel on the car could lock, to prevent the car from going downhill, or be released to allow the car to go downhill and rest the horses. When the aqueduct was completed, most of the line was removed by locals for firewood, and the rock for ballast for area roads.

77. Scholl's Hill

One of the higher hills in the area, this property was part of the 30 acres granted to John Addamson in 1750 which he called "Largo." Louis B. Scholl, son of Henry from the Bunker's Hill house [see page 90], lived here. The house was built c. 1870 and has been gone for many years. In 1900 Louis' sister, Mary E. Scholl Jones, was living with him, with her two children, one of whom was Reginald Bernard Jones.

CHAPTER THREE
THE HISTORY OF MOUTH OF MONOCACY

The area that became known as Mouth of Monocacy was the site of early indigenous people's canoe routes, fishing traps and paths. Used by the Seneca and Susquehanna, the Piscataway's were the last tribe to live here. After leaving Prince George's County and the misunderstandings with the Rangers, the Piscataway set up an encampment here, but were wiped out by smallpox, from a white trader or negotiator.

The first white visitor was Franz Louis Michel, a Swiss explorer looking for veins of silver in 1707 followed by George Ritter from Bern, Switzerland in 1708. Martin Chartier found Louis living here with a Shawnee. The Potomac River winds around horseshoe bend and then opens into the basin where the Monocacy River joins it. The explorer made notes about the area, such as the depth of the two rivers, height of the mountain, and the fishing nets left by the Piscataway. The Bern settlers eventually settled in North Carolina, and called their community New Bern.

Artifacts have been found here from the Carrollton Manor era, 1723-1780. In 1750 William Lucketts operated the ferry at Mouth of Monocacy and in 1751 it was run by William Osborne. In 1781 this area became separate from the Manor when land was granted to Charles Meredith Davis called "Meredith's Hunting Quarters." Here he built Mt. Hope for his bride Sarah Claggett.

George Washington was, among other things, a surveyor. He had surveyed in this area, and remembered it when he began looking for a spot along the Potomac River for the Federal City. In November of 1790 Washington ordered Francis Deakins to make three plats of his choices for the capital, with Mouth of Monocacy being surveyed on November 12. The area had trails but no roads at this time, but there was a ferry for the farmers to bring wagons across the river.

The petition for the road from Bunker's Hill to the Potomac River was answered in 1793. The road was measured off and graded. So at this time the Baltimore Road extended from Baltimore, down through Clarksburg, Barnesville, past Oakland Mills and to the river. The two rivers were deeper then, and navigable by sea going vessels. As farms have been cleared, tree roots that once held soil in place have disappeared. The silt has washed into the rivers, and now only fisherman venture into the basin.

Near the Mouth of Monocacy was a block where slaves were auctioned off. Most were from local folks who were selling to other locals. Advertisements in the Frederick Town Herald began appearing in 1811. Most tell the date of the sale and how many "Negroes" were to be sold. Also were rewards posted for slaves who had escaped.

In The Bartgis Republican Gazette, May 23, 1812 there was a petition to change the path of the Mouth of Monocacy Road. It proposed to 'stop up the road leading across from the Monocacy at Davis's Ford, to open a road from Kephart's Tavern to Roger Johnson's Furnace Ford, then between the the land of said Johnson and Solomon Davis to intersect the Baltimore Road leading to Mouth of Monocacy near the farm of Abraham Jones.' This would place the road more toward Licksville, and across at an angle, taking the path that Dickerson Road has behind Licksville School. This road followed the county line, diagonally, from Martinsburg, but was abandoned following the army traffic which severely damaged the road during the war, and after construction of the Furnace Ford Bridge provided a better crossing.

Other advertisements of the time show gentlemen farmers looking for managers, foreman, and farms for sale. On December 18, 1813 the Charity J. Jones 148 acre farm was for sale at Mouth of Monocacy. The following year Monocacy Mills opened to produce flour. It was operated by Ignatius Jamison and Davis Richardson. Also advertised are moving sales and bankruptcy sales. William D. Hooker's personal property was auctioned at Joseph Kershner's Tavern at Mouth of Monocacy according to the Frederick Town Herald of September 2, 1815. In 1816 a teacher and a blacksmith were wanted for the small community. Other farms in the area were advertised including: John Nicholas' 126 acres in 1818, and Edward Thomas' 100 acres in 1819. In the 1820 tax assessment Abram D. Clopper owned 504 acres of "Meredith's Hunting Quarter."

Isaac McPherson owned and operated Greenfield Mills, just upstream from Furnace Ford on the Monocacy. In order to get enough draft and space for his boats which serviced the mill, the Potomac Company widened the river in 1827 and 1828. McPherson served as the boss of the project. The Potomac Company owned the canal at Great Falls, Virginia.

The biggest financial change for the community came in 1829. Surveys for the Chesapeake and Ohio Canal had been going on for several years, but in March of 1829 construction of the aqueduct was begun. The most ambitious project on the canal, the aqueduct is 516 feet long, with seven 54 foot arches. The first portion of the project was building the first railway to move the stone from the quarries. An in-depth look at this railway is discussed on page 100. The encampment of workers, cooks, foremen, and blacksmiths was there for four years. As raw materials were brought in, stone masons dressed and fitted the stones into their positions.

The initial canal bed and control devices for this section were built in 1829-30. Just above Spink's lock is the waste weir for controlling the water level. The contract for lock 27 was issued in 1828, but actual construction under Canfield and Small began in March of 1831 with the 1828 specifications: Able to lower or raise boats eight feet. Spink's Lock could accommodate a 92' by 14.5' boat with a cargo of 120 tons. After the war, when the canal traffic increased, lock 27 was doubled to accommodate two boats. The breast walls had to be removed and the canal bed was excavated eight feet before the construction took place. In 1875 while the canal was drained for the off season lock work was completed.

Boss carpenters were paid $2.50 a day, and had three men under them earning $2.25 each. Boss masons got $4.00 a day and the five men under them earned $1.50. The blacksmith was paid $1.50 per day. They made hinges, railings and other hardware. The two women cooks in the camp were paid $20.00 a month. Boss laborers were paid by the month at $47.50 with eleven laborers under them.

Each Wednesday newspapers were brought on horseback to the Mouth of Monocacy Store, operated by Frederick O. Sellman. The store also had accommodations for canal supervisors who came periodically to inspect the progress and quality of the work. The flour mill was still in operation, and encouraged that the new canal would ease trade and commerce, a granary opened up as well.

The aqueduct was completed in April of 1833. As the workers moved on toward Cumberland, the make-shift camp shriveled up. But angry farmers were left on the Virginia side of the Potomac. For years they had crossed with their produce and goods to go to market in Baltimore. Now they had no way to cross. They petitioned the Canal Company for several years before a swing bridge was finally installed near the lock-house.

Another of the Sellmans, Gassaway, also was an enterprising man. He bought John T. Tuttle's house and household goods and rented it out as a tenement for $75.00 per year. Several small houses existed after the workers left. One was later used as a boathouse, and others were torn down in the 1970's to keep vandals and squatters out of the area.

The C & O Canal Co. tried to fight the B & O Railroad for many years. After the war, though, they lost the battle. The Metropolitan Branch would run along side of the canal at some points, and not far away for the rest of the miles. With the coming of the iron horse, farmers could transport milk and other goods which might spoil on the slow moving barges to Washington. This area of the line would be section seven during construction. In 1865 surveying began, with construction beginning in 1871 on this section.

The Monocacy Aqueduct was operable from 1833-1924, but it almost was destroyed in 1862. As early as May of 1861, small parties of Union cavalry attempted to disrupt canal operations by destroying locks, breaking waste weir boards, and capturing and burning canal boats. When the canal was drained in November, it became an easier crossing point for Confederate troops. As a result, Union Cavalry were stationed at various points to protect the canal and prevent crossings.

On September 4, 1862 Major General Daniel H. Hill, C. S. A. sent two brigades to drive away the Union forces at Mouth of Monocacy. Thomas Walters heard that the troops were planning to destroy the aqueduct and urged Hill to drain the canal instead, since he could not damage the aqueduct with the supplies he had with them. That night and the next day many locks and canal boats were burned or damaged and a hole was drilled for a powder charge in lock 27, which was detonated. When the canal was drained, the artillery units and supplies could easily cross the ditch on planks. The division marched down Mouth of Monocacy Road on September 5 and turned toward Frederick to meet up with General Thomas "Stonewall" Jackson's troops, who had forded the Potomac and crossed the canal. On September 9, 1862 Robert E. Lee sent Brigadier General John G. Walker to destroy the aqueduct, but his men were unable to drill enough holes in the brief time that the unit had. The damage to the canal from these incidents was repaired by October 14, 1862.

By 1879 the population of Mouth of Monocacy was 20. This included Frederick O. Sellman, merchant, Dr. William D. Hellen, physician, Rufus Bouic, William A. Beall, and George R. Hays.

The network of roads in the area was stimulated by the canal trade and the railroad. But the peak of overland travel had passed. Coal was still being barged down the canal, but the railroad was the popular mode of transportation and transporting goods. The canal had brought more industry to the area, but the small mills couldn't compete with larger mills down county. Many millers turned to farming, growing wheat, rye, corn and establishing orchards.

By this time, too, the canal had seen it's heyday. Boats loaded with coal often burst through the lock gates, destroying them, and spring freshets often caused expensive damage. During the off-season, usually mid-November through March, the canal was drained for repairs to structural damage.

When the season resumed lock-tenders listened for the signal from approaching boats, blown on horns. Each lock had a very heavy iron key to turn the louvered paddles in the gates. This controlled the water flow into the lock. Barges had to be secured in the lock while they were being raised or lowered so that they did not drift up to the gates and damage them. The flume was at the base to handle any over flow, and send it into the Potomac River. When the barge had been raised or lowered, the windlass was turned to open the gates.

Life on the boats was hard, there were constant duties to be performed. Hay for the mules had to be put out for the resting pair housed in the forward compartment, harnesses needed to be greased, and the bow lamp had to be cleaned and trimmed, the reflector had to be cleaned, endless tasks. The mules were often changed while the barge was locking through. The plank was set out, and the resting mules were brought out, while the tired team was unhitched. Having multiple sets of mules allowed for quicker trips and more trips per season.

The flood of 1924 finally closed the canal. It was considered a location for a parkway, but was saved from that fate, largely by the efforts of Justice William O. Douglas and became a National Park. In 1972 flooded rivers from hurricane Agnes damaged the Monocacy Aqueduct severely. It is now reinforced with rods and girders.

Summer cottages sprang up on the banks of the Monocacy near the Aqueduct. These attracted squatters, squalors and ne'er-do-wells and unhealthy conditions. In the spring of 1983 the cottages were cleared out, the trash removed and the lower boat ramp closed off to make way for the new C & O Canal Park. During June of 1998 First Lady Hillary Clinton staged a media event from the Aqueduct with an opening speech about funding to save Historic Landmarks. Perhaps funding for stabilization will someday become available.

Post Masters

James Fitzpatrick	12 Feb 1833
mail service discontinued	
Thomas Trundle	6 Apr 1854
P. O. discontinued	22 Mar 1855
Nathan T. Talbott	17 Apr 1855
Gassaway Sellman	17 Jun 1856
Hugh T. Price	11 May 1857
William Trundle	15 Mar 1859
mail service discontinued	16 Aug 1862
re-established	25 Aug 1862
Cornelius H. Clagett	25 Aug 1862
mail service discontinued	30 Aug 1864
re-established	14 Jun 1865
William F. Sellman	14 Jun 1865
Frederick O. Sellman	28 May 1868
James F. Campbell	20 Jun 1888

discontinued and mail service transferred to Dickerson
15 Oct 1909

CHAPTER FOUR
RESIDENCES AND BUILDINGS IN MOUTH OF MONOCACY

1. Sellman House

Gassaway S. Sellman purchased 227 acres of "Resurvey of Beall's Good Will" and prospered here with tobacco, grains and food for his household in the 1840's and 50's. He employed a school teacher, William Bogle, who lived on the property, as did a large number of slaves. Son William owned the farm from 1865-1872, when his sister-in-law Damaris purchased it. In 1890 the land was sold out of the family. The house later was abandoned after James and Jane Padgett died. Norman and Dora Padgett Wolfe lived here from 1938-1947. The house fell into disrepair at this time and was going to be torn down . Thankfully, in 1948 George W. and Rowena Dronenburg purchased the house and saved it. They added plumbing, a living room, pantry and laundry facilities. Upstairs they took one of the original bedrooms for an upstairs bathroom, and added two bedrooms. The fields behind the Dronenburg's four and a half acres, and across the road are part of the Otto Anderson property which has now passed to Bill Anderson. A house that was located on the property burned in the early 1950's when the Burris family lived there. The stone bank barn is in ruins and over grown with vines.

2. Daniel Price Farm

John Hilton purchased this property c. 1830. William T. Hilton, noted builder, spent his youth here, before moving to Barnesville. Ordered by the Montgomery County court to sell the land, part of the tract sold to Mrs. Mary Appleby. On March 14, 1870, John H. Scholl surveyed the land for Daniel Price, who purchased the farm that year. The adjoining land was a tract called "Jordan." The Offutts farmed this land before Bill Anderson purchased the property. Harry Ensor farms the land now and says that well from the old house still remains.

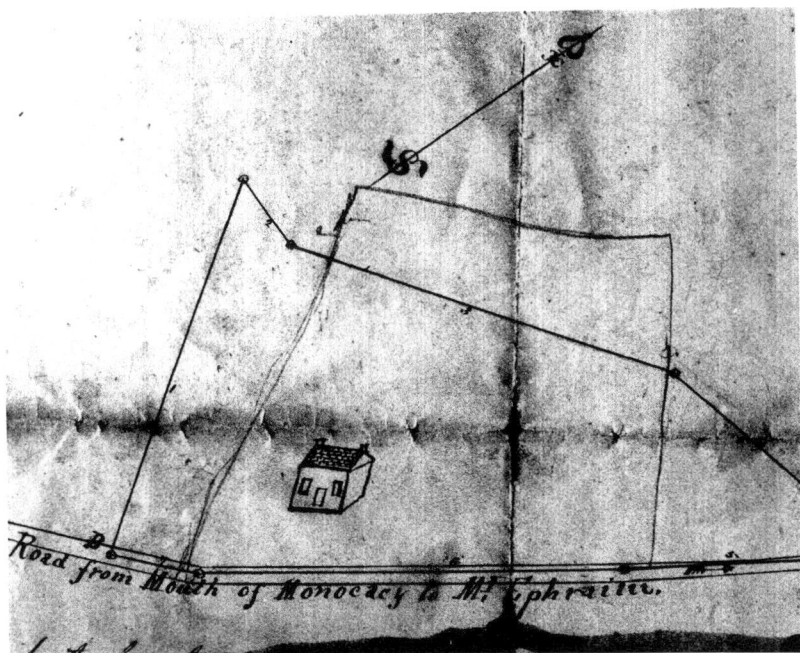

3. Walters-Sellman Store

On the left side of Mouth of Monocacy Road was the store which was operated by George B. F. Walters in the 1860's. It was built on the land grant "Meredith's Hunting Quarters." He was also a boatman on the canal, and jointly owned a boat with Frederick O. Sellman called "Monocacy." In 1870 Sellman took over the management of the store, and purchased it in 1877. His sons Oliver and Ross clerked in the store in the 1880's. Otho Trundle was also employed at the store which sold products to boatman and local farmers. The post office was located inside and Sellman was one of the postmasters. He retired to Dickerson in 1890. Pictured is Lowell Smith, grand nephew of Frederick O. Sellman.

4. Site of the Grain Warehouse and Platform

The foundations of the granary are increasingly more difficult to see. The storage warehouse was located next to the basin for easy loading into the canal barges to transport to the Georgetown markets. The Old Baltimore Road converged here with several other roads on land called "New Harbor." Prior to canal and railroad days farmers took their produce by wagon to the Baltimore markets for sale on this very old east-west road. The ruins of the bridge for the old road are still visible in the winter, and traces of the other two old warehouses that are over 160 years old can sometimes be seen.

5. The Basin

The canal barges were built to be almost as wide as the locks, and therefore there were places along the canal where one could not pass. The basin was wide enough for two boats, and provided a place for loading, tying up for the night and passing.

6. The Aqueduct

Work on the aqueduct commenced in March of 1829 and was completed in April of 1833. The workforce for the project included: sixty Irishmen quarrying at the white quarry; one hundred men cutting white stone; thirty three masons including tenders, drivers, etc.; ten men procuring backing stone at the pink quarry; one boat and five men transporting sand, ten carpenters and a blacksmith. Spanning five hundred sixty feet with seven arches, this structure is a technical engineering feat. The aqueduct was opened with a ceremony dedicating the plaque located at the half way point. On the towpath side, a wide platform carried wagons, as well as mules. Years later Harry Talbott had a shack on the bank where he sold vegetables and rented row boats.

7. Lock 27

Once the site of Spink's Ferry, serving the Virginia farmers crossing the Potomac, lock 27 was built in in 1831. The engineer was an Englishman, Jim Campbell, so this lock was sometimes called Campbell's lock, but more often Spink's lock. In 1875 this lock was extended so that two boats could be raised or lowered together. A pivot bridge was added after area farmers continued to petition for a crossing. The old road bed was on the berm side of the canal. Other lock-keepers here were Thomas Walters, and John Whalen whose wife was found dead floating in the lock. Pictured is a lock-keeper turning the windlass.

8. Lock House

The lock house was built in 1831 and is one and one-half stories over a full stone basement with end chimneys. Built of red "Ashlar" Seneca sandstone, some of the exterior stone was boated down from the quarry. The house is located at mid-lock of lock 27 and upstream was called 'Eight Mile Level' even though the next lock is in seven and one-half miles. Lock-keepers grew vegetables and caught turtles to make soup. Often they traded with boats locking through—some of their cargo for fresh vegetables and blackberry pie. Lockkeeper Jim Campbells' daughter Blanch found a bottle floating in the canal that a doughboy had thrown from his train as he left for camp. In it was his name and address. She later married the soldier who must have had a good aim, Harry Johnson. In the late 1700's Dr. Charles Boyd had a store and still near here, but the remains are no longer visible. The last person living in this area was Norman Wolfe, from 1948-1960.

9. Railroad Bridge

In 1870 a Bollman deck truss bridge was built at mile 37.4 over the Monocacy River. It's three masonry piers were seventy five feet high, spaced two hundred feet apart. Sandstone and quartz stone were quarried at Rock Hall by 75 men, while the limestone was brought from Washington County. The iron sections were manufactured in Baltimore, at the Mount Clare shop of the Baltimore and Ohio Railroad. E. D. Smith was the contractor. The B & O attempted to stabilize the bridge in 1893 with three additional stone piers reducing the span to one hundred feet between supports. During the double tracking project the old Bollman trusses were replaced with the present seven steel girder spans in 1904. In addition to the two-way traffic, the viaduct could now handle the heavier trains. The viaduct is now seven hundred thirty feet long and ninety six feet high, having had concrete block additions to raise the bridge. During World War II soldiers were stationed here to ensure that no one blew up the bridge or attempted to damage the supply route. Three or four armed men guarded the bridge in shifts and their tents were there for the remainder of the war. Passengers can see the aqueduct while crossing the viaduct.

CHAPTER FIVE
OAKLAND MILLS

The Little Monocacy River runs from Barnesville to the Monocacy River where Parr's Ridge bottoms out, Zachariah White established a brick grist mill fed by the Little Monocacy. An advertisement in 1772 listed the new mill for sale. Thomas Morton purchased one hundred acres with a mill at Mouth of Monocacy Road and Baltimore Road in 1783. When he had financial difficulties, he had a co-owner, Ignatius Davis. The operation was expanded and in February of 1804 Davis advertised in the Frederick Town Herald to hire someone to dig a large mill race. A saw mill and plaster mill were located near the brick mill along the creek. In 1806 the mill sold to Joshua Johnson who operated it until 1810. Moses Lugenbeel purchased the complex from Eli Dorsey, Jr. and when he had financial difficulties, William Hempstone became his partner. During this period the mill was sometimes referred to as Hempstone's Brick Mill. Lugenbeel still owed Dorsey money on the mill purchase in 1823 when the case went to court. He was ordered to auction off the mill, but the buyer was unaware of all the liens and the sale was never finalized.

After the war the condition of the mill deteriorated and in 1871 another court case record states that the mill was run down and over grown. The Baltimore and Ohio Railroad purchased the property for the viaduct, and built the "temporary" wooden trestle in 1873. During Leonor Loree's administration, stone replacements were built for several unstable railroad structures. The Little Monocacy Viaduct was raised and replaced with the current triple-arch stone viaduct in 1905-6. It is 331 1/4 feet long, 76 1/2 feet over the Little Monocacy, and the arches are 90 feet high.

Along the road to the mill was Mary Hempstone's house, later used as a store. Just past that was a small stone house where Richard Venable Morton lived until his death. Not much is visible at this site.

The Bethlehem Meeting House was located near here. Basil Berry and Thomas W. Green were preachers here. Zachariah Gaither Harris, Daniel Price and Thomas Mulligan were the class leaders. All of these were later active in the Methodist Episcopal Church. The old log structure was probably built by workers on the old Harris farm, as it is referred to in his 1798 will "to remain open for those in the area." It was in disrepair by 1836, and probably the core of those who met here founded the Barnesville M. E. Church.

Down stream was Daniel Price's mill. In the 1850 census he was listed as a manufacturer, as was one of his sons.

CHAPTER SIX
FEATURES OF OAKLAND MILLS

1. Site of the mill

The three-story brick mill, plaster mill and David Zeigler's saw mill were located in this vicinity. Also a millers house, 40 acres of land, and a cooper's shop. The water table was much higher then. The lower photo shows mules and crews beginning the B & O Railroad viaduct project.

2. The Viaduct

Located at mile 34.9 was a five hundred feet long timber trestle that was seventy six feet above the water. In 1904 when the double tracking project reached this section, a new three arch stone viaduct was constructed and the tracks were straightened. The superstructure was built at the Mount Clare shop in Baltimore at a cost of $300,000. The viaduct was built of sandstone, limestone and white quartzite, the latter having been quarried at the Johnson quarry near Sugarloaf Mountain. The present structure is three hundred thirty-one feet long, and seventy six feet above the water. It is a Montgomery County Historic Landmark.

CHAPTER SIX
THE HISTORY OF SUGARLOAF MOUNTAIN

Sugarloaf Mountain is approximately 17,000 acres, 1,282 feet high and is a dominant feature of the area. Actually a series of three summits, it is an isolated hill, or monadnock. It is listed on the National Register of Natural Areas. There is evidence of Native Americans coming here on their annual migration hunting elk and eastern bison. The first people of European descent to visit the area were traders. Two French fur traders, Franz Louis Michel and Martin Chartier, set up a trading post near Mouth of Monocacy. Chartier was married to a Shawnee. In 1712, when Swiss Baron Chistoph von Graffenried explored the area for a possible silver mine he and Chartier ascended and charted information about the mountain.

The Johnson Brothers attempted to purchase the entire mountain in 1787 when they discovered that 2,000 acres were not included in any grants. Abraham Faw, a former employee of New Bremen Glass Works, and member of the legislature, opposed the bill. A source of fuel in the 18th and 19th centuries both for New Bremen Glass Works and for the Johnson Furnace; the mountain also supplied the superior quality of silica that Frederick Amelung used at New Bremen. Work crews dug the silica along the western sides of the mountain. Trees were cut in sections for making charcoal for the blast furnaces and it took 30 years for the trees in that section to be ready to be cut again. An acre of forest produced 30-40 cords of wood which made 35-40 bushels of charcoal. During the Johnson Furnace's heyday, an acre of trees per day was needed to make the iron they produced.

Charcoal was made in a pit which was tended by a collier. The base of the pit was flat and about 30 feet across, helping the wood to burn evenly. Four foot pieces of wood were stacked in a triangular shape around a wooden chimney and smaller pieces of wood were placed in any gaps, to close off air spaces. The chimney was filled with kindling and before it was lit a layer of leaves and dust was spread over everything to make it as airtight as possible. Once lit, burning was controlled by vents at the base which could be opened or closed. The collier next separated the charcoal that was finished from pieces that needed a longer exposure, and began filling baskets for the wagons. A wagon could carry between 100-300 bushels of charcoal. The charcoal then was housed in the coal house until it was needed in the furnace. When the need for a better grade of pig iron and greater supply was available in Pennsylvania steel towns, Johnson's Furnace closed. When Benjamin Latrobe visited Sugarloaf in 1810, he climbed the mountain and sketched the family of David Moody and their hut. Moody was part Native American and part black. After purchasing his land, he expanded his holdings following the sale of Johnson's forge, and established a community for free blacks.

In 1830 Nicholas Biddle, the President of the Bank of the United States, acquired 3,000 acres of Sugarloaf. In December of 1832 Biddle had Frederick surveyor Willey James subdivide and plat fifty lots of forty to ninety acres each. Local farmers purchased them for wood lots, and some where built on. Thomas Dawson purchased several adjacent lots totaling 162 acres one of these lots, number 49, was purchased in 1834, passed to Benoni Dawson who sold it to George and James Runkles. The Union Army built a lookout tower and signal station here in 1861. Lumber for the St. Mary's Church in Barnesville was supplied from a wood lot owned by William T. Jones [son of John Lewis Trundle Jones]. In 1911 Gordon Strong purchased this lot from the Runkles. David Trundle bought three of the wood lots with 142 acres. Washington philanthropist William Corcoran purchased the summit, a level, tree-covered plateau with sheer cliffs and breath taking views. He never developed the land, and would not sell it to anyone.

Col. Strong was born in Burlington, Iowa and later moved to Boston. He entered Harvard at age 13, graduated Magna Cum Laude at 16, and then studied law at what is now George Washington University. He practiced law in Chicago, as a patent and real estate attorney and then served in the Spanish-American War in Cuba. Strong was visiting his Harvard classmate, Arthur Trail, and while cycling in the area noticed the mountain from the Frederick County side in the summer of 1899. Louise Davis Brosius remembered Francois Darrieulat and Gordon Strong riding their bicycles to her father's farm when she was 13, and asking if they could board for a week or so. She says they stayed about ten days, riding their bicycles daily around the mountain. Mr. Strong remarked that he intended to buy the mountain, at which the Davis family chuckled. Gordon Strong began with a 39 acre tract purchased from Abraham S. Harris on August 17, 1903 for five dollars. Here he spent weekends in the log cabin [now farm cottage].

On one of his trips around the mountain in 1903, Strong met William Warfield who lived in Park Mills. Warfield was a cabinetmaker and stonemason. Strong hired him to do some of the stone work at ten cents a day. Warfield would walk from Park Mills everyday, work all day, and walk back again. Eventually Mr. Warfield moved his large family to the house next to Halstead School, in 1919.

Gordon Strong had an office in Washington, D. C. where he managed his father's land holdings in the District and where he met his future wife, Louise. Mrs. Strong had been the office secretary, and although she did not enjoy the initial weekend trips to Sugarloaf for hunting and recreation, she did have ideas about the future of the mountain and how it should be developed.

The next two parcels were purchased from Thomas White and Reverdy J. Dronenburg. These adjoining pieces were behind Mt. Ephraim, totaled 25 acres. So that the price of the land would not be affected by Col. Strong purchasing so much of it, he sometimes had his secretary or assistant purchase land for him. Giving them several hundred dollars, and having the deed written up in Frederick, he would then have the transaction finalized. He continued buying acreage until he had enough to build his home. When Strong found the lot plat made by James for Biddle, he kept a copy for himself to keep track of his purchases and by 1909 had 400 acres. For a total of $150 he owned a quarter of the Biddle land, and all but six acres at the crossroads plus all of the land north of Sugarloaf Mountain Road, Thurston Road and Mt. Ephraim Road.

When Gordon's father Henry Strong died in 1908 he left an estate of over twenty million dollars in his will stipulating that 6/13 of it go to operating a school for financially challenged boys from the inner city. He purchased land and had the school built, and brought several boys from Chicago, one of whom was Donald McCormack. When World War I began, he volunteered but suffered a pulmonary ailment. After recovering he attained the rank of Colonel in the artillery.

Strong had five separate plans for the mountain developed over the years. The first was in 1912 by Henry V. Hubbard, head of Harvard school of landscape and architecture. The terraced lawn and formal gardens at the mansion reflect his plan.

Another plan was for the summit. The way in which Strong came to own that portion of the mountain is most unusual. He had attempted to buy the summit from William Corcoran several times, and Corcoran always refused. Col. Strong purchased an inexpensive tablet of paper, and had an elderly friend write a letter. He wrote that he was a poor lumberman who needed to secure the mountain top for its chestnut wood. Corcoran, knowing that Strong wanted the land, sold the land to a man dressed as an aged lumberman. Some years later at a Chicago dinner, a mutual friend was seated between Corcoran and Strong. The friend inquired about the summit and Corcoran bragged that he had sold the worthless land with no running water or access to an old lumberman. When the friend recounted the events to Strong, he was told the rest of the story. So the friend asked Corcoran if he would like to meet the man who had the land, and was introduced to Gordon Strong.

The plan of the summit remained a controversy between Louise and Gordon Strong. After dismissing several proposals from architects to open parks or other attractions, he hired Frank Lloyd Wright to design a park that would enhance the beauty of the mountain and harmonize with it's surroundings. Wright came up with a design that included restaurants, movie theaters, a planetarium, spiral observation decks and parking lots. Fortunately this plan was instead used for the Guggenheim Art Museum in New York, not Sugarloaf Mountain.

The fifth plan was developed by Robert Marshall, a leader in the conservation movement and Wilderness Society. The rustic pathways and naturalistic planting reflect his influence. Louise Strong had been right, and leaving the summit natural was Strong's mark on the mountain. The two trails to the summit allowed people to visit and enjoy the mountain, without cars and a parking lot.

Strong began to count the visitors in 1926, on weekends and holidays. That year there were 788. In 1936 there were 16,932 counted and by 1980 there were 50,000 annually.

President Franklin D. Roosevelt had picnic suppers at Stronghold on several occasions, and Harold Ickes, former Secretary of the Interior, notes that FDR attempted to purchase the mountain for a presidential retreat. Strong showed him Shangra-La on South Mountain as an alternative [which became the site of Camp David.]

Gordon Strong established Stronghold, Incorporated in 1946. The first president was James H. Gambrill, Jr. and there are twelve trustees. He penned these lines about the mountain "From out of the long-forgotten past—
Into the unknown and endless future—A monument, fixed, silent, eternal."

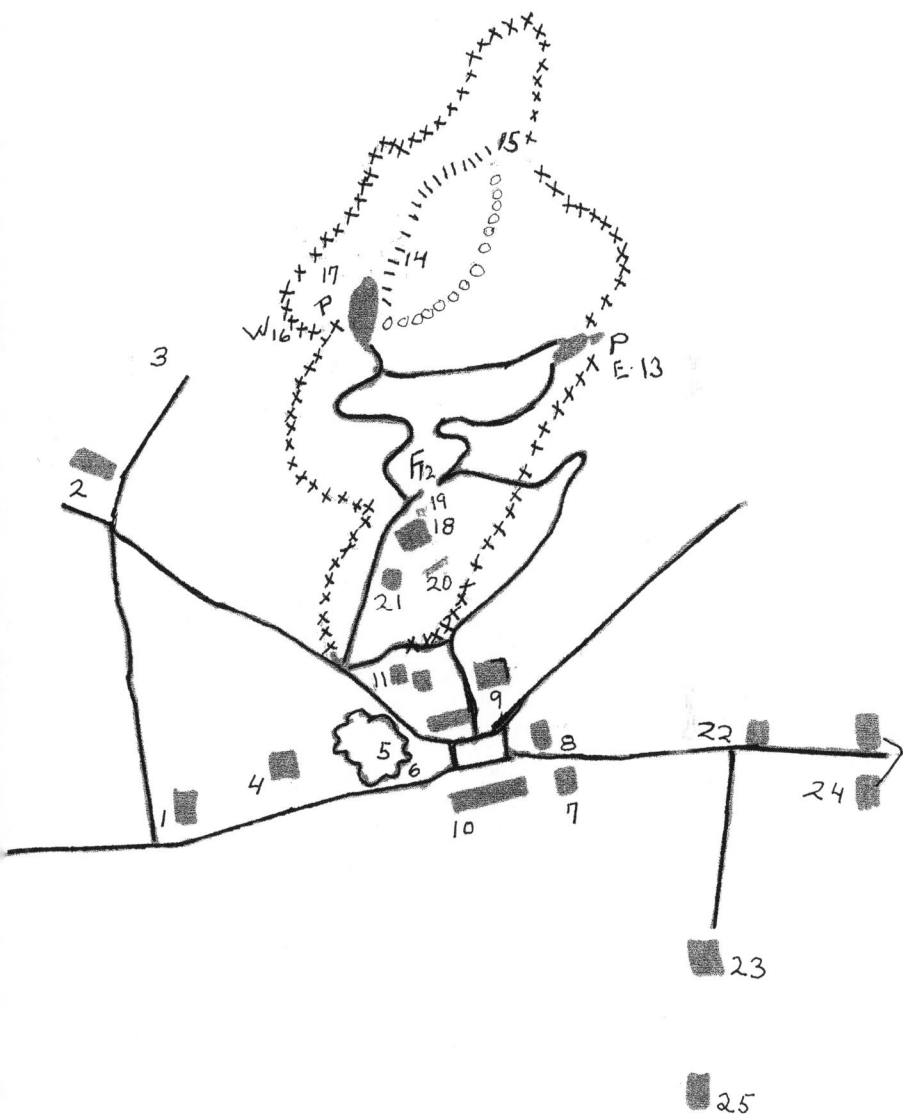

MAP OF SUGARLOAF MOUNTAIN

CHAPTER SEVEN
RESIDENCES AND FEATURES OF SUGARLOAF

1. Beardshire Cottage

Built on "Hopewell" this parcel had sold to Jane Offutt who sold to Bennett Clements, Jr. on November 16, 1819. Lemuel Offutt purchased the property from the estate of James Offutt on July 1, 1833. James Lemuel Offutt sold it to John Brewer on August 9, 1855. In 1916 Lem and Mary Clements purchased the property and Mort Clements lived in this house. In 1918 George Heffner lived here. In the 1920's Cliff and Louise Warfield Mohler lived here. Cliff was a chauffeur for Mr. Strong. Mr. and Mrs. Butler lived here after that. Presently Jennifer Baugher resides here.

2. Comstock School

Gordon Strong's father Henry was once a poor boy, and established a fund that would aid financially challenged students. As part of Mr. Strong's philanthropic goal, he had Comstock School built for the black students to attend. He insisted that Frederick County's Board of Education send a teacher of the highest caliber and supplemented the teachers' salary to extend the school term to equal the white school's calendar. It is a one-room building of frame construction with neo-classical motifs. The school was named after Henry Strong's mother, Mercy Comstock. The school opened in March of 1912 for 26 students with Helen Laud as their teacher. Gordon Strong purchased an organ to encourage choral entertainment and Miss Laud's involvement with the community. The children sat in rows by grade level and attended school from 8:00 to 3:00. After Frederick County consolidated schools, Comstock became the Mount Ephraim Community Center.

3. Mumford's Sawmill

The main industry on the mountain was logging, mostly for charcoal, but also for local building materials. John Mumford's sawmill provided employment and lumber for residents.

4. Farm Cottage

This property was "Hopewell" granted to John Noress in 1724. The grant was for 300 acres. On May 18, 1848 Lloyd H. Nicholson purchased this parcel and lived in this small cabin with his family, which included son Leander, shown on the 1865 map of Montgomery County. The property passed to John T. and Ann R. Nicholson. Edward L. and Naomi Chiswell purchased 107 of the 125 acre tract and sold it to Gordon Strong in 1912. Probably the oldest of the structures in Stronghold, the cabin served as headquarters for the contingent of sentinels for the mountain during the Civil War. Clapboard was later added and the inside plastered. A chimney and fireplace was at each end. The Confederates held the position briefly, during which time the cabin served as a field hospital for the wounded. It appears as though the two rooms of the original cabin were built at different times. This was originally a cabin which rested on rocks at the corners when Mr. Strong had it remodeled by the young architect who was living in it at the time. He had a basement dug, interior crumbling plaster removed and exterior clapboard removed. The rafters were so crooked that Albert Thomas decided a roof would never be seated correctly, so the rafters were also removed. The two log rooms were sitting over a cellar, with an upstairs accessible only by a ladder in the kitchen. An exterior dormer was added for access to the second floor. A new front porch was built using local stones under the foundation. New beams were fitted to support the second floor. The Kessler family lived here prior to Donald McCormack.

5. Willow Pond

There is a spring near the Strong mausoleum that drained toward Willow Pond. This lake was once a rocky field, composed mostly of quartz, where many arrowheads were found. Created in 1910, the road acts as a dam. The lake is a spot of beauty where Mr. Strong could fish and exercise in the row boat. The surrounding land was once called "Hopewell." Granted to John Noress in 1724, it comprised 300 acres originally, but was later enlarged. John's son George purchased part of the property in 1766, but the homestead was preserved and later sold to Elisha Howard, Sr. In the 1820 tax assessment we see that the property had been further divided: Nathan S. White owned 90 acres of "Hopewell," Elisha Howard, Sr., 63 1/2 acres of "Hopewell," and Anthony Lewis 160 acres of "Hopewell."

6. The Fence

Mr. John Dutrow Linthicum and drove a wagon load of students daily from Hyattstown and Comus who were attending Halstead School. While the scholars were in class, he built the fence along four of the roads leading to the square, and others on the mountain.

7. Baxter Cottage

Built on a parcel of "Hopewell" this house was moved in 1914 from the foundation behind the maintenance barn where only a chimney stands. It served as the high school, before the brick building was built. The Warfield family lived here in the 1920's and a kitchen and bath were added at that time. The cottages of Stronghold were named for friends, not for residents.

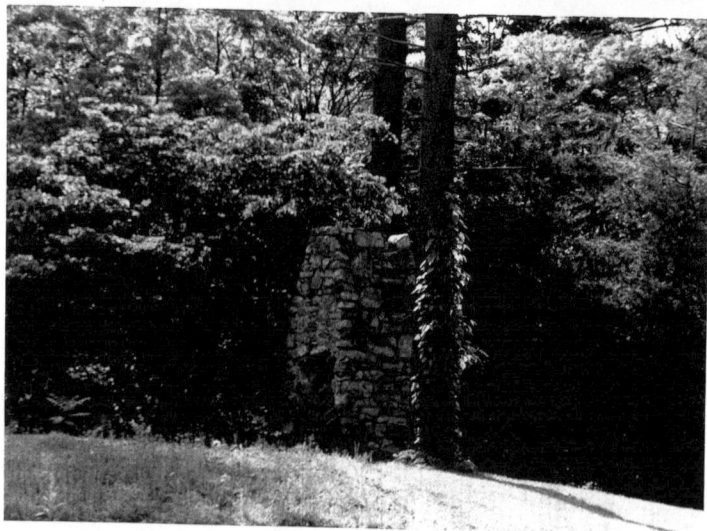

8. Snyder Cottage

This parcel of "Hopewell" was purchased by Elisha Howard. In the tax assessment of 1820 he has 63 acres of land here. He added to this in 1830 and 1833 by purchasing adjoining land. This house originally sat on the stone foundation behind the maintenance building near the entrance to Sugarloaf Mountain. It was used in the 1910s as Gordon Strong's farm home. It was moved to the square in the early 1920s. The house was left to Margaret Greer, Mrs. Louise Strong's niece. After Mrs. Greer died, Mr. and Mrs. Gordon Fry rented it and ran a gift and antique shop.

9. Halstead Frame School

The school house has been located at four difference sites, currently near the entrance to the mountain. It was constructed in 1911 of chestnut, and originally located behind the brick school for boys who Gordon Strong brought from Chicago. In 1916 it became part of the Frederick County Schools when Strong agreed to the pay teacher, Minney Keller. Children from local farms attended, and enjoyed sawhorses on the playground, and privies out back. In 1917 Mr. Fletcher was the principal, with students in grades six though nine coming from Poole's Tract, Dickerson, Barnesville and Comus. Later, it was on Sugarloaf Mountain Road. It was moved in 1991 to the entrance. Present plans include use a museum of Early American School Days.

10. Halstead Brick School

The brick school was constructed in 1917 at a cost of $20,000 to provide a modern facility and courses for students who had been attending the one-room school. The building opened in January of 1918. It was a four-room facility with a basement furnace. Two rooms were for secondary classes, one for junior high and one for primary classes. Blacksmithing was taught behind the school by William and Harold Roberson. Amy Shank, Eleanor Miles and Beulah Jones taught classes at that time, too. Mr. Hawkins, the last teacher, went on to be the president of Towson State Teachers College. Also pictured is a brick from the original wood floor which was wooden block laid in sand. The floor was replaced with wooden planks when the building was renovated for Stronghold, Inc. offices.

11. Vault

In keeping with the other stonework on the mountain, the mausoleum was constructed for the Strongs. Louise Strong died in 1949 and Col. Gordon Strong was born 3 June 1869 and died 26 Feb 1954.

12. First View

This was Gordon Strong's first attempt at opening up the view from the mountain. The road was extended from the original dirt road that had previously ended at the Strong Mansion. The road was paved in the 1930's, but the parking lot was not paved until the 1960's. Many families held picnics around this area when Model-T's were in use and travel became easier. The view faces Barnesville. Just across the road is the old spring with pristine water, it was a treat to many visitors on a hot summer day. Motorists were often seen dipping water from the spring to fill their radiators, as the steep incline caused many motors to over-heat.

13. East View

This overlook was opened in the 1940s and provides a wonderful view of Comus, and on clear days of Gaithersburg and Damascus. Annual Easter Sunrise service is held here, and over 600 attend. The trail that leads to the summit is a more gentle rise to the top than the steps are. Nearby is Devil's Kitchen, were deer are often spotted and grills are available. Ravens and other birds have nesting sites near here.

14. Steps to the Summit

The steps to the summit, as with the other stonework on the mountain was done by William Warfield. He and his crew laid the stones and the projects were supervised by Albert Thomas. Mildred Warfield Austin recalls taking water daily to her father when he was working on the steps when she was a young child. There are two paths to the summit; the hundred steps and the hiking trail. The trail takes a more leisurely winding approach with a gradual pitch.

15. The Summit

Of the summit Strong once said "We believe that, when anyone stands on the summit of the mountain, the sheer cliff hanging over the wild and wooded slopes below...for a moment at least he experiences an inspiration, a moral uplift." At one point in his plans, Strong intended to have attractions at the top of the mountain. Frank Lloyd Wright drew up the plans for a complex that would include a planetarium and parking facility, but the plans were discarded after Mrs. Strong argued for a natural place of beauty. Thus began a nature conservatory and the plans were modified for New York's Guggenheim Museum of Art.

16. West View

The lookout built on the rocks at the elavaion of 863 feet gives one a breathtaking view of Adamstown, Buckeystown, Point of Rocks, the Monocacy Valley, with the Catoctin and Blue Ridge Mountains beyond. Previously the room under the scenic overlook was used to store fire fighting equipment. This area opened in the late 1930's and was favorite place of solitude for President Franklin Delano Roosevelt. He enjoyed going there to smoke and meditate. Picnic tables were designed to deter theft, and the paths around the areas were initially enclosed by rails to maintain the dimensions of the trails.

17. Snack Shack

The snack shack was designed by George Peddicord. It was operated on weekends and holidays by the Pooles of Dickerson. The snack shack is located at the beginning of a circular roadway near the West View. Strong had his crews take great care when designing the roadways, so that they would not be visible from the valley below.

18. Strong Mansion

The location of the nearby spring determined where the house would be built. This spring supplies water to house, and then flows through a reservoir to the barn, shop and other cottages. The mansion was designed to be a main house with two wings, but only one wing was ever built. The Georgian-Colonial wing was designed in 1907 by Joseph Ashe and constructed in 1912 with nine bedrooms, living room, six bathrooms, kitchen, pantry, dining room, and six other rooms. The exterior has one foot thick reinforced concrete walls, with two inches of stucco and eight inch double hollow tiles inside. The walls of the entrance hall have scenes of hill-top houses and castles that Gordon Strong saw in Europe, which inspired him to build on a mountain. His collection of etchings is displayed in the stairwell. The living room which was added in 1928 is paneled in redwood, with teakwood flooring. There are windows on three sides, with two fireplaces on the other wall. Over the mantles are the portraits of Gordon and Henry Strong.

19. Carriage House

Another of the projects by William Warfield and the crew, the carriage house features bays for two automobiles, and a lion head fountain. The fountain was once fed by the spring. The small pool in front of the driveway was once used for bathing and splashing about, since one could not swim laps in it. It now showcases beautiful water lilies.

20. Strong Pool and Garden

Built for actual swimming, guests of the family came to enjoy the crisp, cool spring water feeding into this pool which was cemented over in the 1960's. The terraces and formal gardens are part of the Henry V. Hubbard plan for the mountain and command a majestic view of the valley and Barnesville. The steps pictured below lead to a garden over the carriage house.

21. Westwood Mansion

This Georgian style home was built in 1913 for Mrs. Ella Denison, Mr. Strong's sister. It is one hundred feet in length and features nine rooms. Mrs. Denison's daughter was married in November of 1914 and afterward Mrs. Denison returned to Denver, deeding the house to her brother. After being empty for a while, Albert and Katie Leaman Thomas moved in and redwood siding was added to the outer stucco walls. In 1970 the house was remodeled and the Stronghold Superintendent moved in.

22. Hunter Cabin

This well-preserved cabin was built with interlocking hand hewn timbers and chinked with a plaster and sand mixture. It is two-story and has a pitched roof. The four rooms have windows facing south and a center door. George W. Oden was another of the residents here. Behind this cabin lived Thomas Jones. Thomas Jones, Walter Magruder and O. N. Jamison also lived in the vicinity.

23. Jamison House

The house was built c. 1800 of locally quarried stone. Alexander Jamison's property included 102.7 acres and was surveyed by C. J. Maddox of Rockville. The large plat bordered Elisha Howard's farm to the west, Harvey J. Harris to the southwest, Leonard Hays [formerly John Pyles] to the south and J. Walter Ricketts [formerly Solomon Plummer] to the south, and George Hoyle to the east. In 1909 the adjacent property was purchased from the Trustees of Robert B. Peters. The house is no longer standing.

PUBLIC SALE.

gage deed executed by Alexander Jamison and wife, to the undersigned, dated the first day of November in the year 1867; and recorded in the Land Records of Frederick county, in Liber D. S. B., No. 2, folio 64, &c. the undersigned as Mortgagee, will offer at public sale on the premises,

On Saturday, the 15th day of June, 1872,

at 11 o'clock, A. M. all that Valuable

REAL ESTATE,

consisting of the land described in the above mentioned mortgage; the same being the farm on which the said Alexander Jamison, and wife now resides, situated in Urbana District of Frederick county, about two miles south of the village of Urbana, about one mile from the Georgetown Road, adjoining the lands of the widow Benton, Miss Jamison and Mrs. Trunnel; said Farm contains

156 ACRES,

more or less; the improvements consist of a good two-story Log

HOUSE,

and Kitchen and a good Barn and Stables. It is well watered and has on it an Orchard, and sufficiency of wood for the use of the farm and is under good fencing.
Terms of Sale as prescribed in said Mortgage--CASH.

CHARLES HENDRY, Mortgagee.
I. THOMAS JONES,

May 26, 1872.   Frederick City, Attorney for Mortgagee.

153

24. Clements-Hoyle House

Peter H. and Mary E. Beall Clements moved here from the Rockville area after 1850. They purchased a parcel of land from James Pearre on February 20, 1885 and built a modest home. They raised their seven children here, and daughter Rose B. married George Ernest Hoyle, who purchased the property on October 23, 1907. The couple lived here but all that remains is the chimney and the barn across the road. Arthur and Ann Lee Hoyle lived in the modern house until recently when Walter Avery Snyder purchased the property. A typical barn for this area, the bank barn usually faces south or southeast. The foundation was dug into the hillside, constructed of stone. Livestock were housed on the main floor and stalls ran the length of the barn. Most had troughs in the stalls and hay racks for feeding the animals. The upper level of the barn had a threshing area in the center, with hay mows on each side. The silo stored additional feed, and is a key part of the visual feature of the area landscape.

25. Hayes-Brosius Farm

Located between Barnesville, Comus and Sugarloaf Mountain, this property was part of the vast holdings of the Hayes family. In 1878 Samuel Hayes had a log cabin here, which later was remodeled for the blacksmith and his family to live in. The new home was a frame two-story house, with a front porch running the length of the first floor. A large red barn was reportedly one of the largest in the County at that time. The Charles T. Brosius family moved here prior to 1890 and called the farm "Happy Choice" after the name of the land grant. He built a schoolhouse on the grounds and hired a private tutor for his nine children. On May 8, 1895 the housekeeper deliberately set a fire after the family had retired. The school house, meat house and home burned to the ground. As the children were evacuating the house, they saved the antique grand piano and other items of value. The wagon shed was converted to a temporary residence while the house was rebuilt.

BIBLIOGRAPHY

A History of Germantown Maryland, Susan C. Soderberg, 1988
A History of the National Capital, Bryan
Atlas of Montgomery County, Maryland, Hopkins, 1879
C & O Canal Memories, Lavenia W. Brust, 1970
Circling Historic Landscapes, Maryland-NCPPC
From One Room School to Open Space, E. Guy Jewell, Unpublished Manuscript
Gott Family History, The, Montgomery County Historical Society
History of Carrollton Manor, William Jarboe Grove, 1928
History of Montgomery County, The, J. H. S. Boyd
History of Western Maryland, Scharf, Phila., 1882
Impossible Challenge, Herbert H. Harwood, Jr., Balto., 1979
Interview with Mildred Warfield Austin, D. Cuttler, June 15, 1998
Interview with L. Eleanor Jones Bledsoe, Ida Lu Brown, June, 1998
Interview with Mary Tipton Bodmer, Ida Lu Brown, June, 1998
Interview with J. William Brosius, D. Cuttler, May 29, 1999
Interviews with Richard P. Brown, Ida Lu Brown, 1998-1999
Interview with J. Maurice "Bo" Carlisle, Jr., Ida Lu Brown, December, 1998
Interview with Pete Dilanardo, D. Cuttler, April 22, 1999
Interview with Rowena Dronenburg, D. Cuttler, May 29, 1999
Interview with Fannie Carlisle Ensor, D. Cuttler, May 16, 1999
Interview with Reeva Jones, Ida Lu Brown, September 18, 1998
Interview with Reeva Jones, D. Cuttler, June 12, 1999
Interview with Connie Jones Chesley, D. Cuttler March, 1999
Interview with J. Elmer Hoyle, Ida Lu Brown, June 1998
Interview with Doris Matthews Lewis, D. Cuttler, May and June 1999
Interview with Lynn Lipp, D. Cuttler, April 22, 1999
Interview with Hubert Matthews, D. Cuttler May 12, 1999
Interview with Ross Meem, D. Cuttler and I. Brown, June 21, 1999
Interview with Yvonne Mullgrew, D. Cuttler, July 25, 1998
Interview with Dorothy Roberson Piper, D. Cuttler, May 11, 1999
Interview with Barbara Roberson, D. Cuttler, April 22, 1999, May 16, 1999
Interviews with Ellis Roberson, D. Cuttler, 1998-1999
Interview with Iva Roberson, Ida Lu Brown, July, 1998
Interview with John Roberson, Ida Lu Brown, September, 1998
Interview with Robert Roberson, D. Cuttler, April 14, 1999, June 12, 1999
Interview with Ben Smart, D. Cuttler, June, 1998
Interview with Elam J. Supplee, D. Cuttler, May 28, 1999
Interview with Joyce Wells, D. Cuttler July, 1998, March, 1999 and June 12, 1999
Map of Montgomery County, Martenet and Bond, 1865
Memoirs of Elizabeth Hicks Roberson, Unpublished Manuscript
Montgomery Circuit Records: 1788-1988, D. Cuttler, 1999
Montgomery County Census: 1850-1920
Montgomery County Post Offices, Janet Manual, Unpublished Manuscript

The Met: A History of the Metropolitan Branch of the B & O Railroad; It's
Stations and Towns, by Susan C. Soderberg, 1998
The News, "Quiet Hamlet By The Road" Frederick, April 13, 1963
One Hundred Pages of Comments, Gordon Strong, 1955
Sugarloaf Regional Trails Landmark Research, Michael Dwyer, et. al., 1975
Towpath Guide, Thomas F. Hahn, 1996
Washington Star, "Civil War Echoes Give Montgomery County Color"
December 8, 1935

INDEX

Chiswell, Edna, 48, Edward, 26, 54,
133, Elsie, 48, Hattie, 83,
Lawrence, 6, 81, 82, 83,
Marjorie, 69, Maurice, 47, 82, 83,
Mildred, 47, Naomi, 26, 54, 133,
William, 2
Clagett, Cornelius, 111
Claggett, Sarah, 107
Clark, Jon, 69
Clarksburg, 78
Clements, Agnes, 104, Bennett, 130,
Emily, 25, Lem, 130, Mary, 130,
154, Mort, 130, Peter, 154
Clinton, Hillary, 110
Clopper, Abram, 108
Coates, Marshall, 80
Cochran, Walter, 53, William, 127
Coleman, Charles, 27
Collier, Ann, 104, Beulah, 104,
Grace, 104, Isabel, 104, J.,
, 92,
Mary, 104, Richard, 42, 62,
Ruth, 104, William, 104
Comstock, Mercy, 131
Comus, 1, 66, 80, 82, 88, 135, 138,
142, 155
Cook, Buck, 7
Cooley, Amos, 93, Calvin, 69,
Charles, 56, Claude, 78,
Elizabeth, 93, Herbert, 5,
Louisa, 104, Martha, 56, 69,
Nathan, 12, 47, 59, 104
Raymond, 78, 104, Willie, 58, 80,
81, Zachariah, 56, 69, 78, 92, 95,
Copeland, Oscar, 64
Corcoran, William, 126, 127
Cosgrave, Alice, 93, Charles, 93,
Frances, 93, Joseph, 93, Rose, 93
William, 93
Courts, William, 30
Cox, John, 42
Cromwell, Grace, 58, Richard, 58
Crone, Charles, 69, Kathryn, 69,
Cumberland, 109
Cunningham, Evelyn, 26

Damascus, 142
Daniel, Mansfield, 5, William, 5

Darrieulat, Francois, 99, 126,
Jacquelyn, 69, Marie, 99
Davis, Charles, 107, Ignatius, 121,
Solomon, 107
Dawson, Benoni, 126, Thomas, 126
Day, Piney, 22, 36, 78, Robert, 5
Dayhoff, Lutie, 88, Bob, 88,
Robert, 19, 24, 25, 88, 90
Deadrick, Joe, 60
Deakins, Francis, 33, 50, 107
Denison, Ella, 150
Dickerson, 1, 2, 3, 4, 12, 14, 15, 16, 17,
18, 21, 26, 28, 39, 45, 53, 56, 66,
69, 73, 76, 78, 82, 86, 90, 92, 103,
111, 114, 138, 146
Dickerson, C. Milton, 88,
Christy, 2, 24,
Elizabeth, 11, 86, Harry, 11, 91,
Mozelle, 11, 91, Nathan, 2,
William, 2, 3, 6, 11, 12, 19, 24,
42,
Dickerson Quarry, 3, 42
Dilanardo, Pete, 76, Sally, 76
Dixon, Calvin, 93, Elizabeth, 93,
Grover, 93, Irving, 5, 60,
William, 93
Dorsey, Eli, 5, 121
Douglas, Charles, 30, William, 110
Dove, Arnold, 5, Emmitt, 5
Dowell, Peter, 69
Dronenburg, Dorothy, 60, Ernest, 104,
Franklin, 104, George, 5, 112,
Harry, 5, 39, 60, Reverdy, 98, 99,
127, Rowena, 112
Dudderar, Will, 45
Dugent, Miss, 47
Dulany, S., 78
Duvall, Malinda, 95, 103, Mrs.,
William, 103,

Eaton, Lawrence, 48
Earp, James, 89
Edwards, Catherine, 93, David, 93,
Ensor, Fannie, 18, 102,
Harry, 95, 102, 113
Everett, Annie, 44
Everhart, Harry, 7, 58

159

Mejias, Pedro, 19,
Mellon, Andrew, 37
Michel, Franz, 107, 125
Miles, Eleanor, 99, 139
Miller, James, 93
Mobley, Arthur, 93, Elisha, 3, Frank, 93,
  George, 93, Henry, 93, John, 93,
  Laura, 93, Mahlon, 93,
  Mary, 93, Mr., 19, 68
Mohler, Cliff, 130, Louise, 130
Monocacy River, 28, 33, 35, 107, 120
Montgomery, Infant, 93
Moody, David, 33, 126
Moore, Bill, 83, Clinton, 99
Moreland, Edward, 2, 93
Morgan, Thomas, 78
Morningstar, Annie, 64, Marshall, 64
Morton, Richard, 121, Thomas, 121
Mossburg, Ida, 93, Infant, 93,
  Samuel, 93
Mount Carmel, 30, 50
Mount Ephraim, 6, 19, 82, 98, 99, 127,
  130
Mouth of Monocacy, 1, 6, 31, 107, 108,
  109, 121, 125
Moxley, Mr., 92
Mulgrew, Gerard, 38, Yvonne, 38
Mullholland, M., 78
Mullican, Mary, 90
Mulligan, Frank, 5, Harry, 89,
  Thomas, 121
Mullineaux, Mr. 47, 69
Mumford, John, 132

Nelson, Arthur, 1, 52,
Nesbitt, James, 55
Nicholas, John, 108
Nichols, Charles, 93, Harriett, 93,
  John, 93, Rose, 93
Nicholson, Ann, 133, Arthur, 29, 32, 91,
  Baker, 5, 7, Carrie, 22, Clarke, 5,
  Claude, 27, 63, Douglas, 5,
  Elizabeth, 26, 53, 56, Ella, 27, 63,
  John, 93, 133, Lawrence, 3, 27,
  30, 36, 55, 56, 58, 59, 61, 62, 63,
  64, 67, 68, 80, 81, 82, 83, 99,
  Leander, 133, Linwood, 32, 37, 52,

Nicholson, Lloyd, 133, Susie, 29,
  Thomas, 31, Willie, 27
Noress, John, 101, 133, 134,
  George, 101, 134
Norris, William, 1, 75, 78

Oakland Mills, 1, 2, 95, 107, 122
Oberdorfer, Carol, 61, Michael, 61
Oden, George, 151
Offutt, Elizabeth, 95, James, 130,
  Jane, 130, Lemeul, 130
Oram, Bob, 40
Orme, Charles, 5, 6, 80, Vivian, 80
Osborne, William, 107

Padgett, Algernon, 7, 81, Frank, 78,
  James, 63, 112, Jane, 63, 112,
  Joseph, 64
Page, Ernest, 92
Painter, Elizabeth, 30
Parks, Fred, 46
Parr's Ridge, 1, 2, 3, 14, 121
Pearre, Franklin, 104, James, 154
Peddicord, George, 146, Grace, 86
  Hammond, 86, Thomas, 86
Peters, Robert, 152, Thomas, 5
Phiban, Mary, 27
Piasecki, Daniel, 37, Mildred, 37
Plummer, Mary, 90, Solomon, 152
Point of Rocks, 2, 3, 145
Poole, Harry, 5, Raymond, 5, 58,
  Walter, 63, William, 2
Poole's Tract, 47, 102, 104, 138
Poolesville, 50, 78, 87
Potomac River, 1, 50, 107, 109, 110
Price, Ann, 93, Charles, 93,
  Daniel, 33, 93, 95, 113, 121,
  Hugh, 111, John, 45, 102,
  Joyce, 45, Kathryn, 45, Lawrence,
  37, Lula, 93, Sarah, 93, W., 93
  William, 93
Purdy, Lee, 22
Pyles, John, 152

Rachel, William, 5
Rae, Heather, 83
Rainey, Diane, 78

ABOUT THE AUTHOR

Dona L. Cuttler is a Maryland native who descended from several pre-colonial Maryland family lines. She is a graduate of Takoma Academy, and USC. Her great-grandfather and grandmother started the family interest in genealogy, and local history, and Ms. Cuttler has expanded the project throughout several counties in Maryland.

Other Heritage Books by Dona L. Cuttler:

Montgomery Circuit Records, 1788-1988 [Maryland]

One Man's Family

Paperclips: Selected Clippings from The Montgomery Sentinel *[Maryland], 1900-1950*

The Cemeteries of Hyattstown [Maryland]

The Genealogical Companion to Rural Montgomery Cemeteries.

The History of Barnesville and Sellman, Maryland
Dona L. Cuttler and Ida Lu Brown

*The History of Clarksburg, King's Valley, Purdum,
Browningsville and Lewisdale [Maryland]*

*The History of Dickerson, Mouth of Monocacy,
Oakland Mills, and Sugarloaf Mountain [Maryland]*

The History of Comus [Maryland]

The History of Hyattstown [Maryland]

The History of Poolesville [Maryland]
Dona L. Cuttler and Dorothy J. Elgin

1049553R0

Printed in Great Britain by
Amazon.co.uk, Ltd.,
Marston Gate.